CHANGE STORIES

SUCCESS AND FAILURE IN CHANGING ORGANISATIONS

DR TRACY STANLEY

A catalogue record for this book is available from the National Library of Australia

ISBN 978-0-6486607-3-6 (paperback)

ISBN 978-0-6486607-2-9 (ebook)

Editor Desolie Page AE

❀ Created with Vellum

CONTENTS

DEDICATION

I dedicate this book to all leaders
seeking to drive positive change in their organisation.

WHY I WROTE THIS BOOK

When I returned to Australia following a period of living in France, I was surprised by the emergence of change management roles, and particularly short-term ones. What were they doing and how could they drive deep change in processes, attitudes and culture if they were only present for a few months?

I'd been a dedicated change manager myself, supporting the rollout of a global Customer Relationship Management (CRM) system impacting on sales and customer service staff. I'd learnt a great deal about the challenges of getting people to work differently through the CRM project and was keen to learn from the experiences of others in supporting deep change in organisations.

Why change?

Organisations are driven to change the way they work for many reasons: changing technology, changing customer preferences, new competitors within a global marketplace and changing government regulations. Indeed, organisations need to get better at changing if they are to survive: the average age of a company listed on the S&P 500 has fallen from almost 60 years in the 1950s to less than 20 years. (You can read more about changing survivability rates at www.ft.lk/columns - article 4-653904)

I decided to research and write a book sharing stories from a range of change management programs as I was interested in learning more across areas including:

- Types of initiatives or programs people had been asked to support.
- What activities had change leaders done.
- What they had learnt from the project – both the successful and unsuccessful bits.
- What insights could they share with managers about to lead similar change programs in their organisation.

I also wanted to explore what were the characteristics of the best change managers, and specifically those who had only a short time to have an effect.

Who is the book for?

I originally thought that I was writing this book for other change management practitioners like myself. However, my editor pointed out that the learning was of value to any manager who needed to lead significant change in their organisation. So this is the manager to whom I speak throughout the book.

I've always loved stories. Those in this book are varied, sometimes surprising and always useful. They provide context and learning in a memorable way.

Like many before me I have used the metaphor of the journey to describe a change project. I think it's useful as most change projects have a clearly defined starting and end point.

This book explores:

- What is change management?
- What do change managers do?
- What makes them successful at what they do?

This is how I've organised the book.

PACKING FOR THE JOURNEY

A background briefing on what change management is, what change managers do and an overview of what happens on successful and unsuccessful journeys.

THE JOURNEY

The stories that were shared with me sorted by objective. This wasn't that easy as many change projects had multiple objectives such as changing culture as well as introducing new systems.

AT END OF JOURNEY

An exploration of the journey's end (well obviously) and what was learnt along the way. It explores how to measure the effectiveness of the journey, the characteristic of the best change managers and teams.

RESOURCES PACKED

A review of the resources we took with us on the journey, like our tools and templates, and provides a dictionary for the all the 'changey' language.

HOW I WROTE THE BOOK

To document the learning from successful and unsuccessful change projects, I reached out to 24 people with expertise in change management. They were from seven nationalities, fourteen were female and ten were men. They were change practitioners, project managers, general managers, scrum masters and human resources managers.

This book shares their experience in driving change in organisations and captures what they learned. Their anecdotes and reflections are wonderful, interesting, sometimes funny and always useful. I'm very aware that my own experience as a change manager has framed the way that I've shared their stories. Collectively the contributors have worked on a diversity of change projects across industries including banking and financial services, energy, mining, manufacturing, telecommunications, hospitality, health, higher education, consulting, legal, state and local government, and non-government organisations.

. . .

Some change programs came from state or country-based organisations, others came from organisations operating across a region such as Asia Pacific, and others occurred within a global organisation.

Many of the people I spoke with had international experience in change management in global organisations – adding multiple cultural complexities.

I kicked off the interviews with:

1. How do you define change management?
2. What type of change programs have you been involved with?
3. Tell me about what you learnt from the successful ones. What were your measures? Can you share a story?
4. When change went off the rails: How? Can you share a short story? What were the early warning signs? If you had to do it again, what would you do differently?
5. What are the characteristics of the most effective change practitioners?

While there were common themes/responses which I highlight at the beginning of each chapter, there were also differences. I think the differences are interesting. For example, do practitioners really manage change or simply help people to better accept the change?

I've characterised the stories by themes: mergers and acquisitions; new models and processes; building skills; driving cultural change etc. This was hard as many of the stories touched across all areas. There was richness in every story and universal lessons for all managers leading an organisation through a change process.

When I started interviewing, I initially explained that I was just interested in the stories and not the tools and templates that they used. However, because of the frequency of comments, not only about tools and templates but also about processes including favourite questions, I've added a chapter describing these.

The importance of discussing terminology and the language that we use also became apparent. I've included a section called 'Language of Change' to help those not familiar with change management and project management jargon.

There was common agreement about what makes a successful change project and practitioner. The list of characteristics, processes and competencies is long.

.   .   .

It was useful obtaining insights into when change managers were used and when they weren't, and the impact of not using a change manager.

I loved writing this book. I learned so much from every conversation. My thanks to those listed in the acknowledgments. For reasons of confidentiality, I've not identified who told which story nor have I revealed the organisation from which the stories came. Instead I've mentioned the industry and given every interviewee a new first name.

BIG PICTURE: WHAT DID I LEARN?

My goal in writing this book was to learn more about driving change in organisations. Having worked inside large organisations, I knew how challenging this could be. I wanted to learn what contributed to the successful projects and what were the early warning signs that the project was likely to go astray.

I know that some of you will want to read a summary of insights before deciding if it's worth your time to read further. There's a lot of learning in the pages that follow, but I've condensed it to reveal the nuggets.

The top ten things that a successful change management project and practitioner need:

- Understanding of organisation environment
- Capacity to absorb the project

- Active support of sponsors and opinion leaders
- User involvement in design of new systems and processes
- Sufficient role and process mapping
- Detailed stakeholder analyses undertaken
- Communication and engagement (lots of it and targeted)
- Working closely with other groups including HR, IT and process engineering
- Skills development and coaching of leaders
- Managing within a governance structure.

Projects go astray because of the opposite conditions to those described above. In addition, the project could be focused on fixing the 'wrong problem'. Through the stories shared I learnt more about influences related to organisational history and culture, country culture and political environment, which in themselves could consume many pages.

Effective change agents need many skills, as you'll see by the length of Chapter 19, 'Characteristics of the best change managers'. I worry that a summary disguises the depth of these competencies but will again provide a top ten.

- Relationship development, empathy, compassion and resilience
- Gravitas – credible, self-aware, professional and confident

- Perspective and insights – sees the big picture, is curious and comfortable with ambiguity
- Attitude – has a learning mindset, is innovative and admits mistakes
- Methodology – broad knowledge of frameworks, tools and processes, and which to apply
- Project management – across resourcing, risks and time management
- Understanding data – requirements, testing, traceability and measurement
- Understanding businesses and disciplines – has broad organisational experience
- Communication, coaching and skills development
- Politically aware.

Many people ask what a change manager does. It was this question and the desire to learn more about change management which drove me to write this book. Broadly speaking, a change management role is concerned with the people impact of change (and sometimes processes) as the organisation moves from the old to the new arrangement. Again, I've distilled the learning into a list of top ten.

- Conduct stakeholder analysis and readiness assessment
- Develop plans and metrics
- Run project management office
- Map business processes and roles

- Have conversations with stakeholders and sponsors
- Build leadership skills; conduct coaching
- Run assessments and facilitate workshops
- Collect and analyse data
- Design learning processes and communication collateral
- Track progress and elevate issues influencing success

So that's the big picture, uncomfortably squeezed into a few bullet points. The richness in the detail of the stories is lost in the high-level findings; however, we'll continue as I explain how the stories are organised.

PART I

PACKING FOR THE JOURNEY

L ike many before me, I have used the metaphor of a journey to a far-off and difficult-to-reach place, as a way of framing the conversation around driving change in an organisation.

The book is divided into four parts.

In the first part, **Packing for the Journey**, I explore what change management is and what change managers do, outline the characteristics of the most successful change projects, and provide insights into what is happening when change programs begin to go astray.

The second part, **The Journey – Change Stories**, is where the bulk of the change management stories are shared. We consider mergers and acquisitions; driving cultural change;

ensuring compliance with new regulations; introducing new systems and operating models; and office relocations.

The third part, **At The End of the Journey**, considers what has been achieved and what has been learned. It considers what happens when the change manager leaves, the measures of change effectiveness, what makes the best change leaders and best change teams

Resources Packed is the final part of the journey/book providing information on the tools and resources that are essential for the journey, as well as explaining the language and jargon of the profession.

1

CHANGE MANAGEMENT: WHAT IS IT?

There is nothing more difficult to take in hand, more perilous to conduct, or more uncertain in its success, than to take the lead in the introduction of a new order of things. (Niccolo Machavelli, *The Prince*, 1532)

Change management is not 'fluffy stuff'. (Therese)

I can't start a book about change management without defining what it is. This was of course the first question I posed in my change conversations. I appreciated the different lenses through which change management was understood. Some responses were procedural. Some behavioural. Many were business-outcome focused. You probably have one of your own. Each definition provided an interesting and useful perspective.

Let's explore these perspectives.

Technical and people sides of change

Many change programs are driven by technology, or the new systems are a part of a broader business process and systems change. These types of changes impact on the way work is done; when jobs change, the people effect must be considered. People want to understand why a new system is being introduced, what are the benefits and more importantly, how it will affect them on a day-to-day basis.

> It's really about managing the people in the change. It's not just the people impacted by it directly: it's the project team as well as change management extending for the team. But it's just about managing the expectations, *making sure people understand what the change is, why it's happening,* what it means to them and what they need to do. Lionel

Achieving user adoption

Anyone who has ever introduced a new system will tell you that just because a system has been installed, it does not mean it will be used, or used in the intended way. Users can avoid it or enter the barest minimum of data. This is why addressing the behavioural and skills development side of the change is important.

> You can introduce the best system, process, operating model – whatever that may be – at the end of the day, if people don't adapt and utilise, then you only have half the pie. Carrie

Neil observed that it's more helpful to explain change management framed as user adoption.

> When you're defining change management, I talk about *user adoption*. You can talk about psychology, but at the end of the day it comes down to individuals, or groups of individuals seeing the need for change or being comfortable enough and confident to make the change.

Ingrid echoed this concept.

> For me, change management is about *helping a business adopt new ways of working*, whatever that would be. And for me, it's about *accelerating the rate of adoption*. I'm one of those people who absolutely believes that there will be a dip in productivity, which is absolutely fine. And my job is to try to help *minimise that dip*. The quality of the job I do is the difference between how fast we get people moving and working in that new way.

Change in the status quo

Tomes have been written about politics, power and status in large organisations – not surprising as it's an important influencer. Changes to organisational structure, decision-making processes and even how the office is set up, all influence power and status. Stakeholder analyses undertaken at the beginning of the project need to identify all people affected by the changes and how they are impacted, both materially and status wise. Some of these changes may not be immediately obvious to a new arrival in the organisation.

Taking people from a current to future state

The metaphor of the journey describes movement from a current location to a new location. It has a sense of completely leaving behind the old location and way of working, to arriving at a new destination and new way of working. It's similar in concept to the **Start and Finish** concept on a project. The limitation of this model is that the new way of working may not be completely embedded by the finish date. Indeed, I was told stories of people refusing to use new systems and of slowly slipping back into the old way of working once the project had ended. This learning highlights a limitation of considering a change management project as a **one-off process**, although some practitioners viewed it this way. That's OK because being comfortable with complexity and opposing opinions is what we do as change managers.

> I understand change management to be potentially a *one-off process*, with a definitive start and finish within a controlled environment to deliver a set of specific outcomes and benefits to the end user. Damien

> It's moving people from a current state to the future state with as little disruption to the business and to the individuals impacted as possible. So things like, What are we doing now? How are we going to work in the future? What are we going to do to our processes and structure change? Neville

> It's not just about moving them from point A to point B. It's how they stay there and don't slip back to their previous way of working. Kyle

Process supported by frameworks and tools

There are many methodologies, frameworks and tools developed by organisations such as Prosci and Mckinsey, (to name a few of many) to support the change process. These tools guide the data collection analysis and planning processes; many people understand the change journey through the language of these tools. You'll hear references to...

> *systems, structures, strategy and culture* that require divisions, groups, teams, and importantly individuals to adopt different mindsets and different behaviours in order to achieve a desired objective. Fiona

> Change management uses tools and templates to manage the people side of change. Lyn

> A very *structured approach, and there's a set of frameworks and tools* in transitioning people from A to B. It's really about how they structure the problem. The structuring of the problem could be really understanding and diagnosing what the change is going to be and why they're doing it, through to what innovations are going to take place to help people transition through it. Wayne

Language of change

While the discipline of change management has its own language, change activities often occur in businesses not using this language. Neil shared an example.

When it comes to international development (in Asia), we don't necessarily call it change management. But *change management is a part of everything that we were doing.* Essentially, we were going into a new environment and introducing new educational systems and developing new skills.

I've described different terms used in change management in a later section, 'Language of Change'.

Partnership process

Having a partnership approach to change management describes core values around how the project will be managed, as well as process design considerations.

My focus for *change management is on partnership* and most people do this badly. I'm talking about the sponsor within the business – someone who is helping to drive the change through their team. I can't do it all on my own. Lyn

Building capability

The expression *building capability* is frequently used when talking about change management. It simply means being able to do something. If an organisation can't do something as well as they would like, it's called a capability gap. (There's a nice description of the term capability building at www.brandlearning.com)

.   .   .

Here are insights on why capability building is such a core part of what change managers do.

I very much subscribe to a business-led model of change. This means that the *business owns the change* and that as change managers, we are there to *help support* and *build change leadership and change management capability* within the organisation. This is important because in times of change, people in organisations want to hear from their leaders. Leaders are best placed to help their team members contextualise the change and help people to understand what the change means for their day-to-day role. It is their responsibility to manage the emotional responses to change and they very much set the tone through their behaviours and actions. This is key. It's important that leaders have the skill, mindset and attitude to effectively lead themselves and others through change. In my experience leaders need support in becoming effective change leaders. Leanne

It's a little bit different to project management or other disciplines. I think we're open to understanding what's worked in different environments but every situation is slightly different so has to be tweaked. There are fundamentals that never change. I'm talking about organisational change management and I talk more about the *support and capability uplift* for people. We ensure targeted support and enablement for people but we also have to help them to develop and understand their own capability in a changing work world. Therese

Getting people comfortable with uncertainty

Change often brings uncertainty. While employees will have an interest in knowing how the change affects the organisation, their first concern will be around how they are personally affected.

> *I don't believe that you can actually manage change.* What you can do is *prepare people for the change* and to be enthusiastic about it. I think that our role as a change practitioner is to really get people comfortable with uncertainty. We help the people get on board with process and system changes. To actually define change management as such, the people we're working with have a level of comfort with uncertainty, and be curious about the possibilities of change, and they've got mechanisms, tools and techniques to be able to overcome the levels of resistance and they can move forward to whatever that future state looks like. So, change practitioners should be working with mindsets first and foremost and getting people comfortable with uncertainty. Samantha

Leadership, culture and stepping into someone else's shoes

You'll hear lots of references to leadership being a critical component of any change management program. They describe the vision for the change program and their behaviours are acutely observed, influencing organisational culture.

> Fundamentally change management is definitely not just about managing the product change, or the technology

change. For me, it's about *managing the cultural and leadership change* and embedding that. Oscar

For me it's *pivoting an organisation into a new direction.* Which has implications for people, processes, systems and culture. It's how you give effect to strategy. As I said before, you don't manage change, it's so messy. It's about change leadership. I think that as humans we love stability. Unless you can step into someone's shoes you don't know what it feels like to go through that change. Taking the time to build relationships and engage and try to understand all this from their perspective. Zadie

Directional versus crisis-driven change

While there are many different types of change programs the drivers for change can be broadly categorised into two camps:

Directional driven as opposed to crisis driven, i.e., driven by a change strategy or when the company is in deep trouble. Company could be insolvent or heading for insolvency and is close to shutting down and needs to do something. Nigel

Scope of change management programs

Like all projects, change management programs can vary tremendously in scope. Some practitioners said that change programs they'd been involved with were related to changes that occur across an organisation, although others described the change impact on customers, stakeholders and community members, who were external to the organisation. For others they'd been...

> involved in diverse change programs, affecting only part of the organisation. Irene

> The scope of the project affects time to complete. Merger and integration projects can take from one to several years. Wayne

Pulling together these perspectives, change management can be described in one sentence as a way of supporting a transition from a current to new way of working.

Having looked at different perspectives of what change management is, let's examine characteristics of the most successful change program journeys.

2

SUCCESSFUL CHANGE PROGRAMS

All practitioners want to be involved in successful projects. However, change managers tend to be employed on those projects which are complex and with more potential for things to go wrong. Sometimes change managers are brought in when the project has already failed. I'll talk about learning from these less successful projects in the next chapter, while focussing on learning from the most successful projects here.

From my different conversations, I've learnt that there are many things contributing to a successful change journey. (I apologise for the long packing list.) These things include:

- Solid governance framework
- Deep understanding of the organisation's environment and capacity to absorb the demands of the project

- Good relationship between change manager and client
- Active support of sponsors and opinion leaders
- User involvement in design of new systems and processes
- Detailed stakeholder analyses undertaken
- Tailored communication and engagement activities
- Working closely with other groups including human resources, information technology and process engineering
- Strong professional relationships with key vendors
- Needs-based skills development and
- Coaching of leaders.

So there you have the bare bones. I'll give these bones a little bit of meat now, with gravy and vegies, i.e. further insights, being added in PART 2 – THE JOURNEY. (Hope you don't mind the metaphorical language.)

Governance and leadership

Governance is a useful place to start when looking at what drives a successful change program. But what is governance?

The Australian Stock Exchange (ASX) and Organisation for Economic and Co-operation Development (OECD) talk about governance in terms of the rules, relationships and systems by which activities are undertaken and controlled within an organisation. (All very official sounding.)

I've previously described what change management is in terms of support for transitioning from a current to a new way of working, typically as a project. A change project should have the same clear and thoughtful governance as all your organisation's operations have, with effective governance from the beginning enabling greater speed, visibility and efficiency. Setting up a change initiative without effective change governance can radically slow progress. For example, people may fail to take action if they are unclear about who is authorised to make a decision, or who should be getting informed about key issues. (Anderson & Anderson 2010)

A good governance structure emerged as a foundational element of a successful change management program, as revealed in this comment by Damien.

> If you have a very mature project or program, and you've got an engaged management layer or an executive layer, you've *got to start with governance structures,* including a very clearly identified scope, understanding of constraints and risk, and all those various contributing factors that determine the success of a project.

I like to apply strong frameworks to anything that comes in to a change environment. Because change by itself can be quite dangerous and threatening.

Leadership involvement and decision making are parts of the governance process. Leaders' involvement in the change process was frequently mentioned as critical for success.

> Having active sponsor helps. I think a lot of problems could have been headed off if we'd *engaged the sponsor more*. I mean, there's so much a sponsor can do in a half hour or even 15 minutes. And because of their position, they can open doors. Where change practitioners need to be really clear on is what to ask and knowing that you've got 15 minutes once a week. Let the leader know the one thing they could do that would make a profound difference to your ability to do what needs doing next week. Helen

Understanding culture

The influence of organisational and country culture on people's behaviour in organisations has been the subject of many, many books. Any change manager needs to be able to collect and analyse information that helps them understand the business and culture of that organisation. The larger and more complex the organisation, the more information needs to be collected. When two organisations are merging, you need to double that process when preparing your change management plan.

. . .

Wayne's observations reveal the myriad of cultural considerations involved during a large acquisition.

> There were ten countries impacted by the acquisition. So obviously there's a lot of different cultures and everything because they were an American company. Even though you know there's going to be cultural differences in each of the locations, both companies understood the corporate culture versus local culture.

Because of the scope and cultural complexity of the acquisition, time was spent understanding both organisations prior to development of the change plan.

> At the very beginning we spent time understanding the dynamics of stakeholder groups. We worked with the CEO, his leadership team, regional GMs [general managers] and measured employee sentiment. We did surveys, interviews and really tried to understand where they were coming from – their hopes and the opportunities. Early on this kind of diagnosis was critical. We would have these huge workshops where we just laid everything out, brainstormed and explored what the approach was going to be. Wayne

In addition to culture, consideration needs to be given to capacity, skills development and the order of activities.

Understand the environments in which we operate and the organisation's capacity to absorb the project. Consideration needs to be given to educating project managers about change activities so that we can better understand what happens to businesses during change and of the need to sequence things. Helen

Engagement is key

Activities designed to win the understanding, and hopefully later, the *hearts and minds* of those impacted by the change program, constitute an engagement strategy. Change management programs typically start by mapping affected people and groups and identifying how they're impacted. The stakeholder analysis guides decisions around resources, involvement, communication and skills development activities. It's important to spend time on this analysis, particularly for large and complex projects.

People often comment on my *stakeholder analysis* because I spend time on it. I talk to people such as business analysts and project managers as well as the leaders within the business. I start at the top and at all the meetings I ask every person who else I should talk to. Many change managers don't talk with all the stakeholders. Within the first few months of being in an organisation I will have spoken to all the key stakeholders in the project. Lyn

Key stakeholders should be involved in the design of the new way of working, be that a new system or process or work environment, to both leverage expertise and generate acceptance.

> Have stakeholders involved in the solution, rather than the project or change team coming up with the new processes. We gave them ownership, asking them how it should be designed. Helen

> We had a representative sample of impacted groups, who then participated in the specification of the system and we involved employees from the beginning. Carrie

> People are your most imperative part. If you don't have them on board, you don't have them aligned, you're going nowhere. You cannot do it yourself. It's not possible. I would say that you need to concentrate very heavily on the EQ [Emotional Quotient] on the engagement, making sure people want to do it, they're excited to do it. That they see the challenge and that they are not daunted by it, but are encouraged. Nigel

Getting involvement from influencers, that is people who are perceived as highly credible, in supporting the program is also important for success. They may or may not be senior in the organisational hierarchy.

Having active sponsorship from influencers in the organisation was key. One of the key factors of success was utilising testimonials across each site. For example, one of the insurance brokers was a champion for all insurance brokers. If he was on board, if he was participating, if he was engaging, then all the other brokers would be on board because he had a great level of influence because he'd been there the longest and had the largest portfolio in $ value. Carrie

Change champion roles providing local information and skills development support are often created to support change initiatives.

We didn't call them change champions but influencers. Having those working groups, you can get closer to what people are actually saying and some of them have really good ideas and provides a channel for their voice. Therese

A good relationship between the change manager and their client is a foundational element of a successful change program. Let's explore this important partnership and other core relationships next.

Relationships matter

Trust and a close working relationship between the change manager and their client facilitates ease of access and support for communication and engagement activities. Good relationships with other stakeholders in the organisation are also key.

> Being able to build a really strong personal relationship with the people on the assignment, and then your leadership teams, you know that that is key. And I think having a customer, who is ready to also take some risks and experiment. We work a lot with very short feedback loops, so it's a very design thinking/agile approach. It's almost an intervention or like an experiment, and that has worked well. And we continuously measure perceptions over the following months. Kyle

Depending on the effect of the change program there will be close working relationships with other departments in the organisation.

> Absolutely. HR were involved. IT were involved. Process engineering were involved. Carrie

> Given that we wanted to finish everything within a year we needed to engage with everyone from HR to finance, procurement, sales and all the other functions. And when I look back, a key to success was our early start on building relationships. So even when for example, the finance

departments were so busy that it just didn't have the bandwidth, others were helping. Wayne

The importance of having good relationships also extends to vendors, particularly for technology-driven change projects.

And the other way to distinguish success from not is through a *strong professional relationship with key vendors*. That doesn't mean to say that you go on trips and have dinners. We don't do that. Instead, over time, we have built up a trusted partnership with our key vendors, where both sides have skin in the game. Our success is their success, and we are happy to showcase it as such. This has meant that in times when things are not progressing as they should, we can escalate and get a rapid response and get things back on track. Oscar

Communication

One could easily write a book on the importance of communication during change, with examples of different channels used to broadcast messages. Communication is so important and is often discussed in the context of leadership and engagement.

I've had amazing executive sponsorship across multi agencies at the right level, with people who were incredibly well connected, but we still needed to make the effort to communicate. Helen

Authenticity in communication from leaders is needed.

Employees know if someone is just talking the corporate talk. Leaders can talk through what that change means, and what it would mean for their team. Therese

Change managers can help leaders when conversations are hard.

Conversations are sometimes hard. With an email you get time to think about and answer a difficult question. You don't always have time to think in a conversation. That's OK. You won't always know the answers. You can respond,

'That's a great question and I will get back to you with an answer'. Therese

Here are a few communications activities you could include within a change plan.

Send out newsletters on a weekly or monthly basis as a minimum. Let people know what successes we've had, what challenges we see, what's coming and what needs to be done. We need to be brutally honest. No hidden agendas or secrets – if you possibly can. Nigel

We developed key messages for the executive team to cascade through the organisation and introduced Town Halls. We had an 'Ask the CEO' hotline. We had suggestion boxes and ran focus groups. We updated the intranet, and developed a branded newsletter.

We gave the project a brand – nothing about change – all about *success for the future*. We created a workplace of the future where people could do tours. In a couple of little pods, it would show them that it didn't mean that they were going to be shackled to a desk. Whatever they were fearful of, it wasn't exactly the same as they were going to a different building. They could see what the experience would be like. We used posters, and as many visuals as we could. We changed the screens on people's laptops so that there was a message of the day, week or month. Samantha

Communication processes should incorporate listening and feedback, using onsite face-to-face channels were possible.

Whenever a site had take-up and wins, I shared up. We used Yam Jams on Yammer and would send out an announcement for everyone to go on Yammer right now. 'We're going to have a quick ten-minute Q&A'. We also did as much face-to-face and live interaction as possible. We used roadshows, led by the sponsor and some of our stakeholders, who were our middle managers. They then shared their success stories.

This was a state-based initiative with 18 locations. We did roadshows a minimum of once a month at different locations.

We tried to avoid head office communicating as much as possible because we didn't want people to make the assumption that this was coming from head office. The initiative had come from ground-up as opposed to top-down.

When we picked a location, we would bring in three to four sites which were near, within say a one- to two-hour drive. Participants would drive up for a half-day event and we'd provide food – which was appreciated. Key takeaway here is to have a road map for the events communicated in advance so people could plan to be there. And don't just rely on the manager of the business to communicate about the event. People I relied on at each location included the EA [executive assistant]. They should be at the top of your list as they talk to everyone. And the other person is the administration office manager, as they are the ones who greet everyone when they come through the front door saying,

'Hey, do you know what's happening next week?'
Carrie

These comments demonstrate how to leverage influencers inside the local organisation, which in this case were the executive assistant and administration officer. Giving plenty of notice and making the event more casual and social by providing food also contributed to people showing up.

Email has been a core communication channel in business for at least twenty years. It's fast, efficient and targeted. However, emails 'are not necessarily your friend' as Therese observes:

> I struggle with emails now. People openly share with me that they don't read their emails, wait for a reminder, or decide based on the sender. How do they know that if they are getting an email it's actually something worth reading? How do you use existing channels, like team meetings and other channels that can effectively get the message across? Email is not necessarily your friend.

As a result, she actively promotes other channels for communication of important messages.

> I am defaulting to face-to-face, and considering ways to communicate with four generations working together, that being something we also have to consider due to people's preference. I'm in a division where I have a high percentage of introverts. So how do you give them space to think about things? I don't cut my leaders any slack when they use introversion as their excuse. Sometimes you will have to have some hard conversations with people. You still have to step forward and play a leadership role in change. The division's communication channels include a face-to-face scrum on a fortnightly basis where questions can be asked, and every week there is a director email that goes out with a *this is our week in review.* Therese

Messages shared need to use simple and appropriate language to be effective.

> You need to *use simple and appropriate language* and to *ask for clarification*. I've seen that in a number of cases, where you avoid assuming your definition is the same as other people's. You get insights. You can see that people have a different understanding and you need to take this into account when you're designing interventions. Neil

At the beginning of a change program, communication is focused on listening to stakeholders who may be geographically dispersed. This approach promotes visibility on issues and the consultation process contributes to people's engagement. In the life of a project, things can change. Others need to communicate with change managers regularly to give news of these changes as early as possible.

> It all comes down to the communication. You know, there's so many projects, programs that undervalue communication and they underestimate the magnitude of the change. I think I've made it pretty clear what OCMs [organisational change managers] bring to the table. And unless the OCMs are getting the communication that they need, they'll fail. Damien

I did warn you that there was a lot to say about communication. It's an interesting and important part of change management. As there are many channels available, one could think it was easy to choose the best channels and the right messages. Not necessarily so. The same goes for skills development, which I'll talk about in the next bit.

Skills development and coaching

Change projects can bring change to roles with new behaviours and skills required. A good assessment process will identify the effect of the change so that appropriate learning resources and processes can be created. Resources could include training manuals, cheat sheets or frequently asked questions (FAQs) while processes could include skills development workshops, either online or face to face, and the use of change champions or coaches. That's just a snippet of the extensive list of options. Successful change programs get both the learning process and the timing right.

Measuring outcomes – on time and on budget, however...

Being on time and on budget are classic project management measures for success. From a change management point of view however, these measures are not indicative of user adoption or behaviour change, as Neville points out.

> It was a successful project as everything was delivered on time. All the communications went out, we engaged with everybody and people understood – they knew exactly what their position was with regard to redundancies. Sponsors were also behind the project and the

digitalisation of the records was done on time. The building was a special build and that was done on time too.

This final point highlights the value of having multiple Key Performance Indicators (KPIs) for change projects. These KPIs reflect what success looks like from both business and key stakeholder perspectives. Identifying these at the outset of the project and regularly tracking them will guide actions and priorities as the project progresses.

In summary, the word from folk I spoke with was that successful change programs need active engagement from leaders and sponsors, together with an understanding of how large organisations work, and the influence of culture on behaviours. The most successful programs operate within an appropriate governance framework so people know how decisions are made and resources accessed. Engagement with key people and groups impacted by the change program will ensure their support. Communication needs to be simple messages, shared frequently through the most credible channels for the intended audience. New ways of working often require new skills, so appropriate programs and coaching sessions need to be included in the change plan. Finally, identify the project metrics that most matter and track these on an ongoing basis.

3

WHEN CHANGE GOES ASTRAY

We all have projects in the graveyard to tell the truth. (Erin)

And certainly, those I interviewed had many stories to share with me (as evidenced by the length of this chapter). It's amazing what's revealed by asking the simple question,

What were the early signs that the change program was going astray?

So here are snippets of stories around what most contributed to the change program going off the rails, metaphorically speaking. The first story starts at the very beginning of the project when there's a problem identified.

Wrong problem

When there's a problem in an organisation there's often pressure to find a solution. And quickly. This could mean that assumptions are made and that the root of the problem is not adequately investigated. A solution could then be proposed that only addresses the symptoms and not the underlying cause of the problem. Neil shared his experience in an international development setting.

> I had to shut down a project once, when we had gone right through a tender process, had won the job, and were implementing it. We found out that the project was going to fail. And we had all the pain and suffering around stopping the project when we were three months into implementation. They had the wrong premise and had designed the project without checking some basic assumptions.

Inadequate planning

Planning is essential, particularly for large and complex projects. Many organisations have well-organised change management processes with projects run out of a project management office. This however is not always the case.

> Good change management planning wasn't done. I think the understanding of what needed to be done wasn't really there either. So just a general lack of capability across the project. While we had some idea of who our stakeholders

were, we didn't really manage them or categorise them
properly, understand their needs and probably made a lot
of assumptions around how users were going to react and
adapt. The assumptions are what will kill you every time.
Lionel

At any time, there can be multiple projects and programs
rolling out within a large organisation. We know that every
change project typically has a change sponsor. With
multiple projects rolling out, focus and availability on any
one project can be lost by a sponsor.

Other projects came on board. Other priorities emerged.
Neil

I don't think portfolio management is something
organisations do particularly well. And I think when we
look at portfolio planning, we don't adequately consider
the business changes happening. And we don't look
enough at the organisational capacity.

One person in the room said, 'Well, I've got one
sponsor that's sponsoring 55 projects'. Six to twelve
months later you've got another project with a slightly
different name with the same objective trying to embed
the things that were never adopted because there was
either too much going on, or all the changes were not well
managed in the first place. Helen

The number of projects an organisation is running is typically beyond the control of a change manager. However, they can highlight the result of running multiple projects simultaneously, based upon their knowledge of what successful change projects need and prompt a review of priorities.

> Change can go astray if there are too many chiefs and not enough workers. Hannah

This point highlights the need for adequate scoping of work and clear allocation of responsibilities. We'll look at roles and resources required for change projects in the next chapter.

Lack of leadership

Active sponsor support was identified as key for a successful change project. It therefore follows that absence of this contributes to a project going astray. Gaps in leadership are revealed when: a process is signed off which has not accommodated sufficient end-user involvement; senior managers lack interest in the project and are not available for consultation; there are inconsistent messages; middle managers are not feeling supported from the top; and subject matter experts are not released to work on the technical side of project. It could also be revealed through high turnover on the project team.

If a client is not open and willing to participate in the change process at the very beginning, I think you're flogging a dead horse. Ingrid

I think there are other factors at play and perhaps it comes back to that leadership piece within a lot of these types of organisations. The senior leaders don't necessarily see their role as being pivotal in driving change. It's easy for them to say, 'Yes, we need this. Yes, I sign up for this', and start to take those initial steps and being engaged, but then they kind of take a back step and say, 'I'll let you now drive this'.

I think in bureaucratic organisations that are highly hierarchical, if you leave something to the next level of management to drive and deliver, they very quickly drop it. They just don't feel accountable. They don't feel responsible. They don't necessarily see it as their job. I think, when you're looking at a very hierarchical organisation, you probably need senior leadership more so than in any other organisation. Fiona

Nearly always it's whether the leaders are on board or not. The other thing is if people are really pushing you on $$. I find that if a conversation starts with, 'Here's a massive change program' and they say, 'How much would that cost?' then I can't see that the project is valued. If the leaders aren't on board, if they're not having the right conversations and not prepared to come to the meetings, if they won't give us the time of day to really understand. The change has to be people centred. If they're not up with that they are not for us. Samantha

The only times for me when things have derailed have been when the leadership team or sponsoring team was not *walking the talk*. They say they know, that they're going to treat staff in a certain way, and then they fail to do so. They say they commit to something and then they don't do it. Ingrid

One of the key early warning signs that there might be issues is where the staff on the ground, if you like the technical and the business staff, are having quite a different perspective and a different story to the senior management and the executives. 'This is what we're being told, but effectively we don't believe that because we're seeing something else'. Lionel

More and more it's to do with the ability of the sponsor to have the quiet conversations, and making sure they're ready for change: those two things alone will break you. A part of that make-or-break is the sponsoring, middle management who will make or break your program: they can stop the information going up, and they can stop supporting what's going down, and they can kill it. So you've not got them on board. I struggle to see how you successfully manage change. I put a lot of effort into middle managers when I do stakeholder analysis. Ingrid

So not everything goes as well as it could, and you need to plan your scenarios. The leaders are potentially going through their own change process and their uncertainty is high. How do we keep them on the job? The balance for the leader to process what's changing for them as we ask them to step into leading change, which in many instances is a first for them. Therese

We're kind of in that transition. We've been talking transformation, and that's kind of what's been happening. But there's still this business as usual [BAU], and I think that's a challenge in itself because some of the messages that are sent from the senior leaders are, 'Well, BAU is still important', but we need to do X, Y, and Z to continue our journey. Whereas I think we need to stop that language. This is BAU: this is the new world.

But it's certainly an issue. And what's more, you know, some of the executives could work on their self-awareness. They don't actually seem to see that some of the behaviours and some of the language that they use and how they react (and I use the term react very consciously) to scenarios, actually sends a very, very wrong message.

So they know how to show up at a meeting and you know, talk the talk, but then you go back into the business and that's not always consistent, which is a problem. Probably one of the biggest challenges I see is the us versus them culture. Trust underpins change programs. Leadership messages, and more importantly their behaviours, influence how the people feel about the change program. Support is needed from leaders throughout the program – not just at the launch. Fiona

Politics and personalities

Change managers will need to manage complex internal politics and people with different personalities if they are to be successful. Sometimes politics are visible to all, and at other times they are revealed through decisions that are made. Many of my interviewees talked about projects that they'd been involved with which were derailed for reasons identified as politics and personalities.

There was a personality problem. And that happens. Personalities, politics and egos. I mean, that's the reality of life in large organisations. Neville

Personalities come into play. Mainly because the senior managers were very focused on what they wanted to achieve rather than what the technology could do. Neil

When they've committed to be supportive of a decision, and then they get into the meeting and the big bosses are there and they decide to now be devil's advocate. Because in that moment, they've decided that they could personally get something out of being seen to not agree with this. It's very difficult to be successful in change. People in key positions behave like that, and they will only agree to do things that make their lives easier. And a lot of change does not make people's lives easier. Ingrid

You need to be politically astute There are often more enemies within than outside the organisation. People can *white ant* you. You need to have people watching your back. Nigel

I remember being pulled into meetings, 'Can you just come because you know, I don't want to be in this meeting with this person'. People play nice when I'm watching. A lot of people are very good at that impression management stuff. But it's not until you get two people in the room and there are no eyes on them that you see the true intentions and behaviours play out. Fiona

Takeaways here are that decisions and behaviours are often driven by politics. As a part of understanding organisational culture you will need to quickly understand the politics and have a process for managing them.

Lack of engagement

A lack of engagement with key stakeholders is an early indicator of challenges ahead. It could also be the reason why the change manager was brought on board, perhaps later in the project. Signs that stakeholders are not engaged:

> You could see it on their faces in meetings; disgruntled faces; arms folded; absenteeism. People were disengaged. There was a rise in victimhood, *this is happening to us rather than by us.* No one was thinking 'How can we take this forward and shape it towards a positive longer-term journey for ourselves?' Zadie

> I was called in because there was a morale problem in the IT project team. And after a morning of talking to them I reported, 'No you don't have a morale problem. You have a failed project'. Erin

Understanding the reason for the lack of engagement is important. It's possible that there are multiple projects and that...

> change fatigue is a big problem, along with not identifying the right people to engage. Lyn

It could also be the case that there has been inauthentic consultation.

> There are these digital transformations that I've been through, where they run these workshops, and it's like, 'We really value your opinion', and it's just bullshit. They don't want your opinion. They know exactly where they're going. But they lack the transparency to be honest with you. Ken

Are people engaged and ready to use the new system? It's important that people are ready to use the new system, and that you don't go ahead just because the system is ready.

> There needed to be more conversations about readiness. There needed to be more conversations around 'Are we actually ready to do this from a people perspective?' rather than 'Is the technology ready to sign off?' Helen

The pressurised nature of IT work also reveals insights into why people may exhibit a lack of engagement or show signs of stress on a technology-driven project.

> On a lot of projects you can observe *stress genes*, in that IT can be very stressful by nature, but when you see whole teams, or you know that the majority of the team's behaving in quite a stressful manner, you know

something's probably not quite right. And it's not just a change management thing, but there are other aspects of how the project is being run that are causing it. There's a project manager where I see technical results, unwilling to have conversations with me because they're feeling burned out. I feel they've got too much work. They feel the conversation is going to give them more work and make the problem worse. Sometimes you get what I see as aberrant behaviour, almost deliberately doing things to cause disruption such as *work to rule*. 'Well this is what I've been told to do. I'm doing that'. And it's almost like a lashing out behaviour. Lionel

These comments highlight the importance of understanding cause and effect and of identifying the different ways that a lack of engagement can be revealed.

Change Champions play an important role in supporting change projects as they can bring local advice and training. As key allies it's important that they are appropriately consulted with and engaged in the project.

So the ones that didn't go well. It wasn't one of mine but I had to deal with the aftermath.

You're always grateful that someone provides you with insights from a previous project.

It was quite simple in terms of the division introducing a few systems and they had chosen all these subject matter experts from around the different depots to provide feedback. They were briefed and thanked for taking the role of the subject matter expert. 'Look at this. Give some feedback on the build' – which they did. The systems implemented and like all projects meeting timelines and budgets, it packed up quickly and somewhere in the wrap-up the subject matter experts were identified as the change champion support and for that group of people they reacted with, 'I didn't sign up for this. I'm a subject matter expert'.

The SMEs [subject matter experts] identified with their role and value which didn't necessarily align with that of a champion. For some it was, *I don't feel comfortable with training other people. I don't have the set of skills to be able to do that.* Without a strong champion network, post implementation, the take-up of the systems was excruciatingly slow.

We make these assumptions and sometimes 'change champion' is not the terminology people want to be called or that roles are interchangeable. You've got to understand what your environment is and what it is that you are actually asking people to do. I think that in a highly unionised environment if there is anything that is considered additional work, then what does that mean for them?

I've been on other projects that have had union delegates in their working group signalling that the project is very important for everyone. We are showing that it is important by working with your union representative and that they have a seat at the table.

There were definitely lessons learned around how you get people involved at the right time. Therese

So, the wrap is to look for signs of disengagement and investigate the reasons why. Both stress and failed projects can drive disengagement. It's great to have roles such as change champions supporting the change process, but make sure that you communicate with them effectively and that they agree to the role and all it entails.

Inadequate communication

Communication is a BIG contributor to the success of any project. It's therefore not surprising that inadequate communication contributes to change projects going astray.

> There wasn't any thought given to *why we're trying to do this*. So when I talked to different stakeholders, which is all in our hands, they had very different stories that they were telling. Wayne

> People want to know: What does this mean for me? How does this actually speak to me? What will my future look like? What will I be doing? Why should I get on board with this? And there's still this tension or we're talking about, you know, change from a transformation perspective or BAU [business as usual]. Fiona

In any organisation there are multiple channels available to share messages. Choosing the appropriate way of distributing messages is important, as are the channels for listening to feedback.

A lot of one-way communication or there's been a handful of workshops and there's been no closing of feedback loops and people don't know what's coming next. Helen

Communication needs to be sensitive to country culture as well as organisational culture if it's to be successful.

Thinking about culture here in Thailand, they're more likely to listen to someone high up in the hierarchy because that's the way it is here. They're more likely to do something that's been asked of them by their bosses, than if it was asked by me, this foreign consultant who's coming in trying to tell them what to do.

The training results showed that people needed retraining. Trying to present this to the steering group was a big problem and I actually flagged training as a red risk. With Thais not being happy with negativity, I was forced to change it to amber. And I said, 'I'm doing this against my better judgment'. As a result, they took me off the steering committee, but I was just presenting the facts and the reality of the situation. Neville

Communication needs to be clear and address the interests and concerns of those affected by the change program. People want to know that they've been heard and that their feedback has been incorporated. All businesses need to find a way to continue with business as usual as they incorporate the new way of working.

User adoption missing

There could be many reasons why a new system is not used. A new IT system is often the backbone to a new way of working and is rarely implemented in isolation from other organisational processes. Let's look at two examples of what happened when the introduction of a new system went astray. One was for the introduction of a new practice management system and the other a performance management system.

Practice management system

> The new system was too difficult to use. It was going to slow them down. They didn't have time to send the lawyers on training because they had to achieve their billable targets every day. All they did was pick holes in the technical side of things and it was decided to push back and delay until we had a usable solution. The project failed on launch. Erin

(More on Erin's experience in Chapter 10).

Performance management system

> Organisation mandate was to implement a new, simplified, user-friendly performance system. The sponsor by this stage had pretty much lost interest. Wasn't a fan of performance management. He had in mind an old-fashioned view of what performance management was, not what it could be. And then with the CIO [chief

information officer] in charge of the system, the focus was lost and the focus became *the system rather than what matters – conversations and relationships.* It was an end-to-end IT system, delivered on time and on budget following consultation with a small group of users. Then once it was implemented, no one used it because there wasn't a champion from the business. And people in the organisation didn't know 'Why should I bother with this?' or 'What's in it for me? It's just another thing that I have to do'. Elaine

When introducing new systems, it's important to engage with users in the design process if acceptance of the new system is to be achieved because

People resist things that they haven't been consulted on. Ken

When I think about projects that went were stopped it was because the end user solution was not viable. Lyn

I worked on fairly significant projects as a junior project manager. I didn't have a lot of responsibility and I think our understanding of change management was very immature at the time as we were delivering change in the organisation through new releases to the software system. All sorts of things came out of the woodwork from users saying, 'We had no idea this was going to happen. We expected something totally different'. And then you're backtracking, and you end up with a bit of chaos. Lionel

I was sitting in a meeting last week, and someone brought up a challenge that they were having in terms of trying to adopt new ways of working and being a little bit more agile, empowering staff to actually make more decisions using this new piece of technology. But they said it's very difficult to trust people, because you know, they don't necessarily do the right things and when they struggle, they're not coming back to them and asking for help or support. And so I started to ask questions and talk about strategies that you could potentially adopt. And I don't think this person was aware, but they actually rolled their eyes and looked at somebody else. Oh my God. I couldn't believe it. I was so shocked. Fiona

It's frustrating to get to project end and not have user adoption. This type of outcome points to a failed process from a change management perspective. As has been mentioned elsewhere, a project being delivered on time and on budget is a classic project management key performance indicator (KPI). However, if behaviours haven't changed and new systems used, then the project has effectively failed. Fiona's quote above highlights the influence of leader behaviours and of the challenges in changing organisational culture. I want to explore this more in the next section – culture.

Culture

The prevailing culture in an organisation is a complex influencer on change processes. Culture includes national culture, company culture and the culture created by the behaviours of employees. Culture will influence the design of processes. Here are a few examples of the influence of culture.

Working in an environment where the manager does not share the value of everyone being involved. For some managers, it's shocking to include everyone. Lina

You face cultural challenges when introducing an agile methodology in a non-agile environment. What this means in a non-agile environment is that there is a waterfall effect, which means that you have a clearly defined end state. So when you are introducing change you are underpinned by this as the state. Whereas if you are utilising agile, you are creating the future state on the go. If the environment is not used to being on the receiving end of a non-clearly defined future state, 'All hell breaks loose'. Managers get frustrated because they want to know what the end state looks like. They can't communicate to their team members. So, if you have a command and control, as opposed to an iterative/tiered responsive process, then the two will collide. Hannah

I find that power structures and hierarchies are often a massive deterrent or blocker in the way to getting legitimate change done. So that irresistible, complex urge to maintain the status quo, which is so irresistible and powerful, is a big de-motivating element. Ken

We had a new vice chancellor that had set a whole new vision and strategy and one of the core focus areas was to improve client experience and how the organisation worked together, driving that recognition around 'We are each other's clients'. So, if you're sitting in the marketing department, if you're sitting in the IT department, if you're sitting in the HR department, how the teams within those departments actually interact, they need to be treating each other like clients, providing a great experience, across the university. So that was a massive mindset shift because that kind of language didn't exist. And people and staff didn't see each other as each other's clients. Fiona

Culture's influence can be subtle, powerful and widespread. There are instruments which measure culture mentioned in the chapter **Favourite Tools and Templates**. Additionally, a change consultant's experience across a range of organisations will help them to identify different cultural elements.

Takeaways from when change goes astray

Dust yourself off, have a bit of a laugh. I'm a bit of a crier and the glass of wine if you need to. Helen

As Helen reveals, a change agent is likely to be involved in a project that fails at some point in their career. Expect it. Learn from it and move on. In this chapter I wanted to give you a speedy introduction into the multiple reasons why a change project could go astray. I'll share more of the stories in Part 2 – The Journey.

.   .   .

But before we join the journey, I want to give you more insights into what a change manager does. I know that if you've been reading this book sequentially you would have already picked up a few ideas. But let me elaborate.

4

CHANGE MANAGERS: WHAT DO THEY DO?

I n this chapter I recorded responses to the question, *What is it that a change manager does*? It's important to ask this question as the role varies depending on the scope and challenges of the project and the organisational culture.

What my husband says I do

It's probably only in the last five years that I've introduced myself as a (organisational) change manager. As previously explaining what I do rather than my role name, it avoided the confusion with the IT Change and Release role. I talk more about the support and capability uplift for people. I see that we absolutely have to support people but we also have to help them to develop and understand their own capability in a changing work world.

It's really weird because I've been married for 15 years and after 10 years I said to my husband, 'Why do you keep telling people that I work in HR? I have never worked in

HR for the entire time of our marriage. I've worked in change roles for nearly 20 years'. 'I don't know how to explain what you do,' he replies defensively.

'And yet my girls who are 11 and 12 are quite happy to explain to people that I'm a change manager. They use more language around support and helping people. We had to have this challenging conversation around this as it puzzles me that you've never known me in HR – that was a world before'. I think sometimes that it's other people who can't explain what you do, and this includes leaders. Therese

Keeping a finger on the pulse

As a change manager, my role involves meeting with every single division, some of them every week. There are ongoing conversations and constantly being aware of what's going on, really unpacking it, really reading people, drawing themes together, and understanding from a program perspective what could be impacting some of those responses or reactions. And then looking at what we can do next. Fiona

Elevate issues and opportunities

For significant enterprise transformations, it's key to success who you report into. We get a lot of autonomy here and we get to talk to a lot of people to truly understand the sentiment towards change, and any themes and insights we can elevate up to the leadership team for consideration and action. We discuss opportunities or what is going to hold you back if you don't do something about it. As change managers, we rely on our relationships to be effective in our roles. That is the relationships of the people we directly report to as well as our stakeholders in the business or the project teams. So it's a balance to ensure you maintain confidentiality and the trust in those who provide information to you, whilst still being able to elevate solutions and observations in a constructive way. Leanne

Building the change leadership skills of managers

We're co-designing and facilitating a change leadership program for 42 managers as one of the ways we're building enterprise change management capability. We need to support them and build their change leadership. We do self-assessments and coaching sessions to help embed the learning. We've set up a change champion network and we get insights from people at the front line. A big thing for us is our data and insights from our people and using these to inform our change approach, or able to elevate them to the right people. We very much position ourselves as coaches and enablers and facilitators, not doers. Being clear on roles and responsibilities is important here. Leanne

Facilitating conversations. Supporting prioritisation

We're facilitating conversations within leadership groups, building that shared understanding of the transformation and helping them to work through the changes this means for their business areas. I think that the value that a change manager can bring is in terms of facilitating conversations and connecting people together so there's common understanding and we're all working together towards a shared goal.

And something we're doing here is helping the senior leadership team in terms of visibility of all the transformation initiatives coming down the pipeline to support them in their prioritisation. Leanne

Supporting leaders to be comfortable leading through ambiguity: being in the grey space

For many large-scale digital transformations, the focus is on building minimal viable products [MVPs]. This means you are delivering a functioning product early, and testing, learning, iterating and improving on that product as you go. This means you don't always have a full appreciation of how a product or initiative is going to change ways of working or an individual's role until you start using it and exploring future potential of the products. This can be a big change for a business if they are used to being delivered a fully functional end product. In addition to that, we are living in a world of constant change, where being change responsive and adaptive are critical. In modern day organisations there is a lot of ambiguity, and as change managers, we are in a position to be able to support leaders to be effective in leading their teams through change when you don't necessarily have all the answers. Some of the things we are doing is to make visible what we know, through the development of integrated plans and timelines. And providing coaching to leaders on how to manage self and others through ambiguity. As leaders, you're not always going to have the answers, but you need to be able to be comfortable in acknowledging this and be able to lead your team through that ambiguity. Leanne

Strategic change, process reengineering and running the PMO

I've been involved in change management programs for the last 10 years and usually do strategic change. But my very first job also had IT and business process re-engineering. I've met other change managers who basically run project management offices [PMOs]. Ingrid

Coaching and support: not performance managing your staff

They somehow think that a change manager uses the dark arts to change people's behaviour and I have to remind them that I'm there to facilitate, coach and support. I'm not there to do other than the change management function piece. So that means I will never be line managing your people. Good or bad news should always come from a line manager or the manager once removed. Like it or not, a difficult performance management conversation with your staff about their behaviour is also up to the line manager. Ingrid

Readiness assessment, communication and training implementation

If organisations want to implement a new application, a new type of software, or change from the current way of working to a new way and using a different system, my role is to make sure that when it's implemented, the people are ready to work with what's being implemented without too much disruption. So I'll communicate with them. I will work with the sponsors, I'll do stakeholder engagement. I'll look at process changes. I'll look at organisational changes. I'll help with the training implementation of the training program. I'll do business benefits management. And I'll do business readiness, adoption and usage measurement. Neville

Understanding the dynamics of stakeholder groups

I was working at a mobile phone manufacturer based in Singapore, and I was working across the region. We were integrating a very large company that was worth a few billion dollars. We had to integrate this company in one year. In the US multinational company [MNC] world, one year is the expectation. I found that in Australia they take a couple of years.

When you think about change, everyone always talks about the change curve and how that's going to be this valley of despair, to expect that employees will not be productive through the integration process. But it really depends on what you do and it's actually not the case that it has to be like that. Some of the things I found that worked on that project was beginning very early on – we spent quite a bit of time to understand the dynamics of stakeholder groups.

Working with stakeholder groups, with the CEO, his leadership team, regional GMs and assessing employee sentiment, we did surveys, we interviewed with senior managers, we really tried to understand where they were coming from, what were their hopes and the potential opportunities.

Early on this kind of diagnosis was critical. And I think the second thing we did was quickly work together to have a large-scale, co-working brainstorming series where we have these huge workshops, where we just laid everything out and actually talked about what the approach was going to be. I haven't seen a lot of that happen in Australia, but I know it's quite common in US companies. Very early on there are large scale workshops involving different layers – it's not just managers – so that you really want to involve the staff. And I think looking back, this is essentially what we would call a very agile approach. Wayne

Role mapping is important activity in a change process

Even though I considered the project to be successful, we probably still *underestimated the role mapping component.* We understood the process mapping, but we probably undercooked the role mapping so we didn't properly understand the magnitude of change in the various roles. Damien

(This story is expanded upon in Chapter 7 – Decommissioning legacy systems).

Lead by example by being change responsive

As change managers, it's important to lead by example and be responsive to change ourselves. Many times I've worked on programs of change that have experienced big changes themselves. Whether that is a new program director coming on board who has a different approach or a different remit, or an organisational restructure which means different reporting lines for yourself or your business stakeholders. This is all very normal in today's business world. It's important that you remain professional, and do what you can to support the organisational objectives and outcomes, even sometimes if you don't necessarily agree yourself with the changes that are being made. It's important to remember sometimes to focus on things that you can control and influence, and the big picture. This will make you a better change manager. Leanne

I know that reading this chapter is a bit like listening in on a focus group: many different voices, experiences and perspectives. I hope the comments highlight the diversity of change roles in organisations and the myriad of things impacting on the change manager's capacity to deliver. Some of these snippets are elaborated on in Part II – THE JOURNEY to provide further context. In the next chapter I look at those projects that don't need a change manager, or perhaps just need a very 'light touch'.

5

I DON'T NEED NEED A CHANGE
MANAGER WHEN...

·

Some change only requires an email and a cup of tea. (Erin)

I love this quote, highlighting the light touch that some projects require from a change management perspective. For some projects, a little bit of communication and training is all that's required for success.

It really depends on the size of the change program and the type of impact on systems, processes and behaviours. As a result...

sometimes when upgrading systems or perhaps the size and magnitude of the end users, determines if a change manager is employed or not. Damien

Determining if a change manager is needed is assessed during project planning.

> I'm planning a project that's seen as a fairly significant technology project. However, it's not seen as having significant change because we're not introducing any business process change or changing people's way of working. Essentially the technology change will improve the system and make it a bit easier for people to do their job. That's the idea anyway. So it's seen as having a low level of impact from that perspective. Lionel

So that's enough of the high-level descriptions about what change managers do and when their expertise isn't needed. We're now going to look at some of those change stories I promised you at the beginning.

PART II

THE JOURNEY - CHANGE STORIES

I'm writing this book during the time of the COVID-19 pandemic when we've seen governments attempting to get their constituents to change their behaviour and use new systems like tracking apps and adopt new behaviours, like washing their hands more frequently and practising social distancing. This book is not about societal change but there are things we can learn about how messages have been communicated, systems introduced and incentives provided for people to behave in new ways.

Getting back to organisational change journeys, the stories I share in the coming pages are classified by objective. This was harder than I first thought as many change projects, particularly the larger ones, have multiple objectives, for example, the introduction of new operating models, office relocations and cultural change programs. The first stories relate to merging and restructuring organisations.

6

MERGING AND RESTRUCTURING ORGANISATIONS

Mergers and acquisitions combine two or more companies who may have different products and services, cultures, systems and geographic operations. The objective of the merger could be to increase market share and / or reduce costs by achieving efficiencies. A merger can bring many challenges and is often stressful for managers and employees alike, with concerns around changing the way of working, job security and possible relocations.

Acquisition of a company in a previous monopolistic position

We were undertaking a merger and acquisition [M&A] project as a part of a consortium, with a big consulting firm managing the technological part, a range of industry specialists and we were there as the change team. The organisation being taken over had been a monopoly and this was about to change.

We worked across employer relations, and that is often where it starts with M&As as there's a high risk when you can't change work models.

The due diligence phase took around four to six months. What worked particularly well was that we were there from Day 1. We reviewed the workplace being acquired, the people there and had time to understand what the future business model would look like.

We developed a 'What's happening for the first 100 days' plan. During due diligence, we were with other members of the consortium, undertaking analysis and pulling data. Then, once the actual change program started, I brought in with me a team of three. While I worked closely with the consortium, I sat with the leadership team in the acquired company and got incredibly close with them, building trust.

Later I brought in a series of experts – coms [communication] and engagement people – who undertook the more structured change management activities such as an office relocation and introduction of a performance management system. We also had a HR expert who worked directly with our employee relations expert because we had to change policies, procedures and the code of conduct.

Elements that worked well were that:

- We were there at the table from Day 1 and seen as an equal contributor.
- We were also able to take away some risks that the organisation was worrying about. They knew that competition was coming into their industry and their level of readiness was low, creating a lot of fear in the workplace. The employees knew

that they were not up to speed, and that they were not servicing their customers properly.

- Finding internal talent was an early priority and we then partnered with them.
- We gave them insights into what a future state would look like.
- We introduced a rewards system.
- We ran town hall meetings.
- We reviewed the office layout.
- Throwing away old coffee cups as a symbolic gesture towards a new start. We actually purchased new crockery and glassware, it linked (in colours) to the new brand and was a symbol of a fresh start and also in investing in our people so they were not using old chipped glassware, i.e., it was a bit of a step up and it had a positive impact. Samantha

Here's another story of restructuring, this one at a bank.

Major restructure at a bank

There was a major restructure for a bank where we actually let go over 3000 people. By the time I was involved in implementation of the restructure, a lot of work was done already by a HR person who was driving a lot of the initial planning and unfortunately, there wasn't a lot of consideration from a change management perspective. By the time I got involved, it was a bit of a disaster zone. There was a lot of planning around the usual processes for briefings and allowing employees to provide feedback and then a lot of the standard HR processes. However, there wasn't any thought given to, 'Why we're trying to do this?' So when I talked to different stakeholders, they had very different stories that they were telling me. We know we cannot go to the business with their different stories when the core team isn't aligned. And to be honest, we had to really negotiate to push back the project to get our ducks in order. We needed to do a series of workshops to align on why we're doing this. Messages were

Yes, it's about cost savings, but it's also an opportunity for the bank to redefine the operating model.

And that was the big part that was really missed: the design required to work thru the operating model versus just going through the processes.

So basically, I had to put out fires with stakeholders who were getting confused around what was going on with the timing, the why of the change, and just general reservations and nervousness around the operating model with questions that were never really resolved. There wasn't a structured approach to get the whole group to come to an agreed model. Wayne

I heard other stories about change programs in banks where the driver for change was new legislation. Here's one of these stories.

When the 'Why' of the change isn't clear

It was a regulatory project where we were implementing what was required for this insurance company to be compliant. There were two different things to be done: a set of documentation reporting and process changes. And so they had to roll out a new system and a new set of processes. As a result, I had to re-jig the team structure a bit. And I was involved halfway into this project. But the feedback process was very clear. The systems went very smoothly, although there were some technical issues, but that wasn't an issue.

The biggest issue was the market clarity on why we're doing things because how we communicated it was very factual in terms of what the regulatory bodies wanted us to communicate but that actually didn't tell a story. Helping to translate that in a very layman way was really critical but was missed.

The key learning was doing enough testing of messages to different groups of people. Because of this the project selected one team to test. And the other teams didn't have the same impact. So that was why that was the biggest learning from the project. The 'why' just wasn't clear, and because the 'why' wasn't clear, it led people trying to work around the process. They'd been working in the same way for 20 years. And you know, for that part of the business they weren't used to a lot of change. Wayne

The next story is also from the banking sector and describes challenges when creating new systems post-merger.

Merging four onboarding systems into one at a bank

A merger between several banks created the need for an onboarding project, which is the process when you come along to the bank and want to open an account. Every bank ~~has~~ had a different onboarding process. They decided to create one onboarding process amalgamating four systems into one. The system was unbelievably complex with 400 fields for data to be entered with information about 100 products.

I brought in a technical writer to try and map it all and they became completely lost. You can imagine trying to write a training manual so everyone goes through the process the same way. You find you're going to page 3 if you are onboarding the customer from one bank and their products and then to page 60 from another.

The problem was the tool. I'd done my impact assessment, stakeholder analysis and change management plan. I did a training session with the business analyst who had designed~~,~~ the onboarding tool and we were training one of the banks. The second field to fill in was their email address. Immediately, we discovered that there weren't enough characters available for the length of this person's email address. We were stuck before we started. It took me two minutes to identify that this tool would never work without significant rework.

It can be very difficult to be a naysayer in an organisation saying that this is not going to work – when everyone is trying to get it to work. You need to be careful as you get a reputation for being negative and difficult. Anyway, they eventually canned the project. Lyn

Key messages

- Use a structured process to get input from key stakeholders on new operating models.
- Explain clearly the w*hy* for the change and the expected outcomes. Typically, there are multiple outcomes expected from a change program.
- Make sure the core team is aligned on messages.
- Know that there are personal risks in being the bearer of bad news on a project where it is not possible to succeed.

7

DECOMMISSIONING LEGACY SYSTEMS

A merger or acquisition, introduction of government regulations or the emergence of new technology with enhanced functionality could necessitate replacement of existing systems, which are typically called legacy systems. It could also be that it's an older system lacking flexibility or that it's no longer supported by the vendor. The replacement could involve a complete cutover, or a longer phased out approach to protect historical data. Decommissioning legacy systems can be complex and expensive. And they're often not an organisation's top priority.

Change management objectives for these types of projects typically include supporting a smooth transition from the old to the new system. There could be new processes to be developed and both staff and customers need to be trained in the new skills. The next story comes from the rollout of a new organisation-wide platform.

Getting funding for the 'soft stuff'

There was a US-based, global project, decommissioning a series of old legacy systems and processes and adopting a corporation-wide SAP [Systems, Applications, Products] solution, providing a new, secure, safe, supported and stable platform.

There were expectations around the company using this as a lever to move forward. The definition of success was broad, and if I was to put a very loose percentage on it, the actual success of the technology itself, as far as when you actually cut over to the new environment, would probably be 25% of the overall definition of success.

So, all the other stuff, the other 70 to 80% of your success criteria, is more on the soft stuff, those things that are very hard to measure. And it takes quite a few years to be able to conclusively say that we've achieved a full measure of success. And this was a company that was traded on the New York Stock Exchange and it had government and military contracts in place as well as transportation contracts. So it was a very sensitive environment and there were a lot of legal probity considerations.

It all sounded very complicated when it started. We identified a successful partner with experience implementing large SAP-style projects. There were all the various particular project and program resources applied. The impact analysis identified that it was going to be a significant change to the user environment. So while the technical lifecycle was in good hands, and was set to run a successful journey, it became evident that the soft stuff, the end-user stuff was significantly underestimated in this particular project.

There was a lot of effort applied to convincing executives that this hadn't been considered and that additional budget needed to be found. A significant amount of organisational resources were needed for dedicated trainers and system specialists as there was a lot more involved than just giving users system training. There were a lot of processes that happened behind the scenes applied to the new system.

So we needed to bring a whole fleet of organisational change managers [OCMs] onboard and do extensive, process mapping exercises across the organisation.

[So who was doing the process mapping?]

There were the business analysts, but we also had system specialists and nominated representatives from the organisation. We had the ability to share that knowledge throughout the organisation up front. It was quite a convoluted process and it was delivered late by the BAs [business analysts]. We understood what the changes to the workforce were going to be as far as new resources. With the role mapping, we needed to make sure that they kept pace with the process mapping. We needed to understand what the new resource requirements were going to be. Therefore, HR needed to come on board. And then once we got to the end of this process, the OCMs were able to work with the end users and start taking them on the journey with the support of HR and we ended up getting there. I mean it was a bit of a catastrophe at go live because it was a global system with a big bang style of approach.

While the cutover technically was great, it was the end-user soft skills that we struggled with. With the support of

OCMs we were equipped with enough skills to be carry these. And that was successful.

[Can I ask you two questions? You said you recognised that you needed greater support for this and so you asked for budget.]

We hadn't nominated representatives from all the various countries. The corporation was broken up into regions, which was Asia Pacific [APAC], Western Asia, UK and South America. We nominated representatives in the regions and asked them to do an initial impact assessment on the changes. And as soon as the results started coming back in, they were all pretty much just red, red, red. Fear, fear, fear. Scared, all that sort of stuff. So that's when we had to start applying more thought to it.

[How did the OCMs work with the users?]

That was obviously quite challenging because it was a global project. We spent, we exhausted a lot of finance rotating the OCMs from their own regions in through US. They'd come in and spend 2–3 weeks in the US and then go back to their own regions. These were the lead OCMs seconded to the project in the US. They were doing a fly-in, fly-out for 10 or 11 months and we'd set up a series of workshops, and set objectives for them to achieve when they were here and they'd take that back to their own region.

I've learned they'd go out and get a whole new set of questions and then bring that back and then we'd work through the questions. We had lead OCMs in the US that were managing this particular process. It was all very structured and tiered.

[What else was critical for success?]

Well I think it all comes down to the communication. You know, there's so many projects and programs that undervalue the importance of communication and they underestimate the magnitude of the change.

[Any other learning?]

From an OCM perspective, I guess that even though I considered it to be successful, we probably underestimated the role mapping component. We understood the process mapping, but we probably undercooked the role mapping as we didn't properly understand the magnitude of change to various roles. Damien

Key messages

- Seeing a large project as just a systems implementation: you've got to consider the full end-user impact.
- Underestimating the importance of role mapping as well as process mapping.
- Constantly collecting feedback and modifying your approach as required.

8

INTRODUCING NEW WAYS OF WORKING

In a global marketplace, organisations are constantly looking for ways to increase their competitiveness. Their employees, often with deep knowledge, industry relationships and specialised skills, are considered key business assets. As a result, leaders look for ways to leverage their collective human resources to achieve competitive advantage. I know that the term *human resources* sounds like *jargon* and can have negative connotations with people described in the same language as plant and equipment. I needed to use it as it's a common way managing people was described by my interviewees.

Human resource objectives for change projects include explaining the individual impact of change, getting staff buy-in for or acceptance of the changes, managing redundancies and relocations, and ensuring staff have the skills and confidence to undertake new ways of working.

The first story in this chapter looks at changes requiring new skills for call centre staff. The second looks at the introduction of a new knowledge management system in government.

Failed project – When new skills were not properly identified

I have a great example of going into an organisation where change had already gone off the rails and I was asked to fix it. It was a recovery project. I remember coming in and being told that I was change manager number three on this project. And I thought, 'That's nice'. I was told that '90% of the call centre were on stress leave. And we don't know what went wrong'. I breathed in. I was given a pile of documents from the previous two change managers and told to go fix it.

I put the documentation on my desk and asked them where the call centre was. They told me there were a bunch of temps working there, and that it was off-site. I said 'OK. I'll go there'. I did what a lot of people don't do, and physically went to the location.

Let me give you some perspective on this team. There were 32 call centre operators, predominantly women, aged between 35 and 60. They'd been working on average 10–15 years in the organisation. Out of the 32, there were still 10 that were working there, while the rest were on stress leave or were temps.

I was directed to the ten people that were not temps. I asked them 'What happened?' I sat down with them over lunch and they told me it was a new system. I asked them when they got the training for the new system.

'We got training a week before go-live', and I thought that that's pretty good. Nothing wrong there. And I asked them about the training. They said,

'It was all OK when we were using the system and receiving all the calls.

When it started to get difficult was when we had to make calls'.

As a result of this change, they went from receiving inbound calls to making outbound calls. So I asked them, 'What sort of training did you get to make outbound calls?'

'We didn't'.

I went back to the needs analysis and saw that no training for outbound calls was identified. There was however a script on how to do outbound calls. That was interesting because when customers ring, they don't follow a script. I soon realised that they needed what I would call soft-skills training, which covered conflict resolution, styles of calls and how to make calls for people who may have English as a second language. So once I realised that they didn't have any of this sort of training I went back and put my recommendations forward. I then got together with the training team, developed these modules and rolled out the training.

Out of the 32 current staff, 30 were back at work and their confidence went up, because suddenly they had what I would call *competence* again. Two employees were not keen – their concern was justified.

'Look, I have been working 15 years on inbound calls and I don't care to make outbound calls. I'm happy to take a package and leave'.

[What about the call centre manager?]

They quit. Because they couldn't deal with the staff members. Fingers were pointed at them. They became the scapegoat.

[This must have been a great win for you?]

Yes surprisingly. It might have seemed like a no-brainer, but when you miss something like that – this is not just systems change: it's a new operating environment. You should never make assumptions about people's skills. They were highly competent people who were working in an inbound environment for many years. Suddenly you turn that round and you need a completely different skill set to go outbound. Carrie

The next story of change comes from a government organisation when a new way of capturing and sharing knowledge was introduced.

Engaging someone resisting change

A central UK government department was implementing what they called *Open Government*. What they were trying to do was make ministerial briefings available to the general public. Any briefings that were created within a government department, the MPs [Members of Parliament] would raise in the Houses of Parliament. These, they were saying, should be made available to the general public.

What the government embarked on is what they call the Knowledge Network. Each government department had a project to create within their own department, a way of managing briefings in a central repository that would go out from the department into the Knowledge Network, and then eventually to the general public.

Each department had briefing authors and briefing approvers. They had a private office that reported into the minister, and all of the other communications departments had a say in how a briefing was authored.

Briefings were typically authored in isolation of each of the departments within the bigger department. They were all created in different ways. What they wanted to do was standardise the briefings under certain bullet headings covering what's the purpose of this and what are we trying to do. So they created a central repository with a succinctly formatted briefing structure.

Briefing authors would then use that format to create their briefings and upload it into the central repository where it would be approved by whoever needed to approve it, and eventually made available to the minister via his private office.

Given the nature of central government and even local government, they were very much change averse in the UK. One of the internal departments I was working with refused to use the system. They said 'We're too busy – we don't have time'. They refused to engage. There was no agreement to attend meetings. They flatly refused to use the system and didn't attend the away-days and communication of events. It was a problem. So, I put my thinking cap on and said,

'I know you've refused this but, can you give me two hours of your time on one of your departmental meetings within the next couple of weeks?'

After visiting the head of department a few times, they agreed. I personally created a briefing and I uploaded it to the system and when I went to the meeting, I said,

'Okay, let's look at a day in the life. You have a briefing. And can meet the folk from the process where the briefing was requested'. And to cut a long story short, when I showed them the brief that I had created, they looked and said,

'Are you sure you created this? Didn't you speak to any of our briefing people?'

'No I just created this brief based on the information I have available.' And they thought that was awesome.

'So if I can do it, somebody who is not a briefing author, somebody who has very little knowledge, someone with the necessary knowledge should be able to do it in a quarter of the time'.

As a result of that meeting this department became the most prolific user of the new system and in terms of the quality of the briefs, they were far and away the best quality ones out of all of the different departments that used the new system.

In relation to this I can remember a comment by author and change thought leader, John Kotter, who said, 'If you get somebody that's totally change resistant don't bother with it. Just go around them and do whatever'.

I actually disagree with that because what happens is if you actually convert change-resistant people, they become the people that others look up to and become the change advocates. Neville

Introducing a performance-based funding approach

I was working in a largely government-funded organisation, employing 14,000 where there was an initiative to move towards a performance-based funding approach. This approach was counter to the prevailing mindset that we're doing public service work so should be funded regardless of our performance and that successful departments subsidising poorly performing ones was absolutely fine. So that fee-for-service model, it was thought, 'We can play around the edges with it, but we should be funded by government as a whole organisation despite our individual department performance outcomes'.

This spawned an internal review where each department had to give an account of their service and delivery in relation to the funds they received. The project wasn't well sold and there was a huge outcry. This was an organisation where performance was always viewed collectively and never at a divisional or departmental level contribution. There were extreme discrepancies amongst those who were customer facing. Some were very successful with what they did and had a huge revenue base and others were cost centres for business, subsidised by the performance of the successful departments.

The *why* behind this change was never really explained, so there was a great outcry. It was like having your departmental performance review posted on a wall for everyone to see. So not only was it rejected, even by the successful departments, but it became such a confronting approach that it threatened collegiality and created an unpleasant workplace culture. You could see it on their faces in meetings: disgruntled faces, arms folded, absenteeism. People were disengaged and there was a rise in victimhood. Zadie

Key messages

- There is value in converting your most resistant stakeholder to an ally.

- Spend time on your stakeholder analysis so that the impacts in terms of funding and status per group are clearly identified.
- Explain the *why* for change. *(Yes, I know this has been said before).*

9

INTRODUCING NEW OPERATING MODELS AND PROCESSES

A change in business strategy necessitates a review of a company's operating model, i.e. how products and services are created and delivered to customers. As a result, there is often an organisational restructure undertaken when strategy changes. Organisational restructures facilitate changes in perceived status, roles, skills needed and processes. Google dictionary defines a process as *a series of actions or steps taken in order to achieve a particular end.* In organisations, we create new operating models and processes so we can work more efficiently and with higher visibility. Everything an organisation does from an initial prospect enquiry through to delivery of products and services to a customer can be mapped and is typically reviewed when structure changes. Other changes can be driven by objectives for being more customer centric or for creating a safer workplace.

Summary of stories

Stories shared in this chapter include creating a new customer commercialisation division, using Six Sigma to achieve process improvements, changing cash management processes, and introduction of drug and alcohol testing.

Establishing a customer commercialisation division

My role was to set up the customer service division requiring the merging of a number of different teams across field services, technical staff and customer-facing staff dealing with customers on the phone. It was difficult bringing together disparate groups into one team. They all struggled to understand why they were being brought into a centralised customer group, particularly the field services team.

So I focused on helping that team in particular. I went out in the field with them every week, spending time one on one with team members, in order to understand their world. I would ask lots of questions and get to know them as individuals – who had grandchildren and all that. We had this personal relationship. And at the end of that time I was able to pull the whole group together at their worksite, and say

'This is what I've seen and this is what I've learned'.

And that resonated. They knew I'd been listening.

[What had this group been afraid of with the change in structure?]

They were afraid that people wouldn't understand what they did and it would not be valued in a new team. They were worried about their ability to do their jobs well and that was really important to them as they took pride in what they did. By taking the time to get to know them individually and peppering them with lots of questions about their work before the change happened, they felt heard and less apprehensive about the merger.

We also let them work out their own 'new ways of working' in the new team structure. Their manager and the whole field team held separate workshops where they broke down all their processes, exploring what they did when they were in the field, highlighting how onerous the paperwork was. They then looked at ways to make their work more enjoyable and more efficient. They used this organisational change as an opportunity to restructure 'how we do things'. Zadie

Using Six Sigma to achieve process improvement

We worked with a telecommunications company, using Lean Six Sigma improvement projects. They had a really big commitment to use Six Sigma with a large group of practitioners. They had a project going along great guns until they got to the implementation – then the whole thing fell apart. The project affected a number of business units and used the DMAIC methodology, which is a data-driven quality strategy used to improve processes. It is an integral part of a Six Sigma initiative, but in general can be implemented as a stand-alone quality improvement procedure or as part of other process improvement initiatives such as Lean.

In the early design stages, the project was going very well. They got to the implementation side of things and were looking at making changes across different business units, when the whole thing fell apart. They couldn't understand why everybody had suddenly lost interest and were not available any more. The senior leaders who commissioned the project weren't involved any more. There was conflict. That was when it went off the rails.

The warning signs included:

- Senior managers lacking interest in the project and not being available
- Subject matter experts not being released to work on technical side of project
- Turnover on the project team. This is a classic warning sign with a changeover in project directors, project managers and project staff
- Senior executives and project sponsors not showing up to steering committee meetings and not being active on the project. They are what we call a sponsor in name only. 'Write the email and I'll send it out under my name, but no I'm not available to come and talk to the project team. I'm not available to sort out the turf war between this business unit and that business unit'.

Also, there was a

- Lack of involvement of HR, OD and recruitment, learning and development
- Lack of cooperation
- No budget for change management
- Lack of integrated planning between change management and project management.

In some projects, the project drives everything, and change management has to fit in. In other organisations you see change managers and project managers collaborating together to do a single, united and integrated plan. The change manager is contributing to discussions around subject matter experts being released on to the project, to help with the solution design. There needs to be change management before that happens: you need to get the right people released. A warning sign is that the project plan is over here and that the change management plan is over there. Erin

Getting support from the leadership to help staff with uncertainty

I was consulting to a client where the operating model was changing as they were going to new territories. It was a state-based organisation and fifty per cent of the business was actively restructured and relocated. They weren't flipping the business model per se, but changing it by putting customer and stakeholder experience at the front of everything they did. They were receiving a fair bit of negative media because as a gas organisation, there were environmental issues.

[Were there changes to roles?]

Yes. Definitely not just a change of leadership. There was change to roles. It was how we do business. It was an operating model change that happened to have a major restructure associated with it.

[Why was it successful? What were your measures?]

We delivered it within the timeframe that needed to be delivered. Funding was secured. We demonstrated that the changes were in place. We retained the talent that we had identified as needing to be retained, and we didn't get any negative pushback in the media. We were able to sit at the executive table with the sponsors who said, 'You guys equip us'. They said yes when we needed to send out a letter with their signature.

[What was their experience of these types of changes?]

The exec had a HR background in operations so absolutely understood what was needed.

[What else contributed to the success of the project?]

Decisiveness and fairness. When decisions were made, those impacted were respected and treated with a consistent process. Once the decision was made it was quite rapid. People weren't left in a state of 'I don't know what's happening to me'.

Restructuring within large organisations is huge and the impact is different per person. There's not necessarily a collective experience as some people are impacted more than others.

The same with mergers and acquisitions. Just getting them comfortable with uncertainty when it's large and complex. It's not just new roles and new systems and a new language: it's also preparation for doing things differently. Samantha

A change story involving the outsourcing of services and process reengineering follows.

**Introduction of a new cash management process in a
multi-national outsourcing company**

I was working in a company that provided services to large
companies and governments who want to outsource
services, similar to SERCO, which had 28,000 employees
on a cash management project which directly impacted
4,000 finance and business development staff. (A SERCO
style company provides services from operating prisons, to
cleaning schools, to running shutdowns on major public
utilities to providing services to defence).

I was in the change management function with a more
senior practitioner above me and a PMO [project manager
operations]. The objective of this project was to improve
the cash management of the organisation. It involved huge
amounts of process reengineering as they sought to
simplify and make their processes more efficient.

By way of background they had had a huge number of
acquisitions that hadn't been fully integrated.

Keys to success on this project were:

- **Investment in engaging the impacted
  stakeholders,** getting their input into how the
  processes should be. We went around the
  country, running workshop after workshop,
  conducting interviews and communicating via
  online channels such as email.
- **Not assuming we were better than those using
  the current systems.** They do this every day and
  they know those systems way better than us.
- **Making sure that they had a single point truth**

in a data warehouse so that we were all looking at the same figures.

We engaged in a big intelligence gathering exercise finding out where money was going to see if there were any blocks, things like accounts receivable against your accounts payable.

I was always taught to do it before you break it up into the parts of an operating model. So assets, finances, organisational structure, organisational behaviour, leadership, what I call parts of the wheel. And you need to look at each one of those and see where they are impacted and then rate the impacts. If you do a proper business impact assessment, not only do you get a great risk register, but you also understand what barriers you have to reduce or completely ameliorate in order to make sure the change is successful.

This was the first time we'd done a big change program. And we did it properly, all mapped out, with a case for change, business readiness assessment, all the change plans, tech strategy, and communications plans. They were really well documented. Ingrid

A very different story of organisational process change comes from a government agency introducing drug and alcohol testing.

Drug and alcohol testing

A lot of organisations were drug and alcohol testing at that time, and some of our staff were visiting other sites, such as suppliers or partners and were required to be tested, but we weren't doing it on our site. Our motives for going down this path were driven by safety and by keeping up with industry best practice.

We got incredible backlash when we started, with employees saying,

'When we started here 20 years ago, we didn't agree to this'.

We had some parts of the organisation that were very much against it and some parts that just didn't care. It was very polarising. In some areas there was an underlying suspicion that we were trying to get rid of the workforce. And, you know, if we had a beer tonight and came to work tomorrow morning, they'd be going.

'What right have you got to interfere with our time off?'

There was a lot of education required helping people understand what the process was going to be and what it actually meant. We had to reinforce that this wasn't about penalising people or prejudicing people because of personal choices they made outside of work hours. It was about safety in the workplace. And we were one of the few organisations in the industry who weren't doing it.

We implemented a zero tolerance for drugs and followed the road rule guidelines regarding blood alcohol levels.

We needed to provide a lot of education around what the process was going to be and we relied on senior management support for the policy change. There were also offers of long-term support and assistance for those who had difficulty modifying their behaviour. Irene

Irene's story reveals that, if the rationale for changes is not clearly explained, employees make inaccurate assumptions.

Key messages

- Spend enough time with affected staff to better understand their concerns, and the scale of behaviour change required. It will also help you to identify incorrect assumptions they may have made. And stating the obvious: time spent with staff, listening to them, builds trust.
- For big change projects undertake a business readiness assessment as precursor to the development of a comprehensive change plan.
- Be concerned if the change management and project management plans are not aligned.
- Explain the rationale for change, respond to employees' concerns and provide education and support for those who have difficulty modifying their behaviour.

10

NEW SYSTEMS AND DIGITAL TRANSFORMATION

C hanges in technological capability are driving rapid change within organisations because technology can radically improve the reach and performance of an organisation.

The cloud has enabled data mobility with cameras and sensors connecting everyday items to the internet. Additionally, robotic process automation is eliminating jobs while artificial intelligence is creating new roles. (You can read more about digital transformation at www.cio.com – article 3404876).

The pace of change in organisations is driving a digital transformation where digital technology is integrated into all areas of the business.

Change management objectives for these types of projects are broad with behavioural, cultural, process and technological components.

Stories in this chapter cover: when a system is selected for technical rather than business impact; when a new system isn't used in a legal practice; when a new system is pushed through too quickly; and when there's been no end-user involvement in system design.

Consider business fit as well as technical fit when choosing the IT solution

I'd been discussing with Oscar a number of digital transformation projects running in a government agency when our discussion turned to assessing projects for fit.

> We had an example as part of our program, where we had a critical decision that had to be made regarding one of the solutions. The initial mistake that we made was looking at this evaluation solely from a technical perspective, as opposed to considering business factors. Specifically, 'At our stage in our environment, with our needs does this particular solution fit that?'. From a technical viewpoint, this solution ticked all the boxes.
>
> However, on review of the evaluation, our organisation although comfortable with the technical assessment that was done - including the governance, probity and procurement -was not comfortable with the solution considering the business risks that it presented.
>
> We then completed a further assessment, this time through more of a business lens. That review found mostly red flags while the technical solution was rated green. So we went back through the procurement process and back to market to find the right solution for our business.

When the new system isn't used

I heard many stories about new systems not being used.
Here are a few.

> I've seen many change failures because often we get called
> in after the failure to do it again. One of the early ones in
> my career was in a law firm. They had spent two years on a
> technical solution for a new practice management system.
> If you think about law, a practice management system is
> one of their core tools of trade, because you have been
> assigned to work on an intellectual property matter.
> Clients are not going to pay you five hours finding out
> about precedents in your own firm on an intellectual
> property matter in another state. They expect that you are
> able to access files and precedents. And if you are away on
> holidays, clients don't want to wait days to find out where
> your executive assistant filed the documents.
>
> It sounds obvious. But again, at the time everyone was
> used to working in their own way – in their own practice
> management system.
>
> This organisation spent two years designing and
> developing the solution. It was resisted, not only by the
> lawyers but by the admin staff. And interestingly by their
> own management team.
> *[Why?]*
> It was too difficult to use. It was going to slow them
> down. They didn't have time to send the lawyers on
> training because they had to achieve their billable targets
> every day. All they did was pick holes in the technical side
> of things. The project failed on launch and it was taken off
> the computer network and put into a cupboard.

[*So everyone was just using their old system?*]

Yes. Everyone went back to using their personal systems. Erin

A similar story follows.

When a new and inappropriate IT solution is pushed through

I was allocated to a discrete part of advice transformation. It was part of the organisation's much wider advice and information program. Interestingly this was their first agile project which had gone incredibly well. They had integrated online advisors. I was brought on specifically because I could bring the wealth knowledge overlay, understanding what the end users would see or feel. *What they'd built was not fit for purpose.* And they had wanted to push this through quickly because *a very senior person had promised that this would be done by a certain date.*

But I had to help reframe the concept, and confirm the analyses were appropriate. And to make sure that the minimum viable product [MVP] was absolutely appropriate in a very short uptake entering the test to learn, because the 'test to learn' was not just with anyone: it was with incredibly well-connected stakeholders who were a part of the advisory commission. They were like a subset of super advisors who the company would work closely with, who we socialised higher concepts with, as part of governance.

But there were absolutely conflicting needs within the business in terms of pushing it through and getting it done. And I was being very open and honest with my feedback – that if this was pushed out it wouldn't be very well received. And a lot of the things that the organisation was promising were very much under-delivering. They also had a few legacy issues as well where the company had rolled out this piece of technology, and pretty much within a couple of months of rolling it out had to bring it back in, and I could see them pretty much doing the same thing again.

And there was this huge reputational piece. And this is what I see as one of the key components of change and which more change managers should take ownership of when we work hand in glove with the project manager. Because if we're doing our jobs properly and doing that really early analysis to understand who the end users are and what their needs are, to ensure that the program is delivering, and it's appropriate and that it's going to be sustainable and fit the needs and is not going to be dumped over the fence. That's all very fine and well but this is not going to help us and they'll just revert back, to their old habits and behaviours, wasting a huge amount of money, time and resources.

[If you could do it again?]

You would get change involved a lot earlier. I think that they were not driven by the needs of the end users. They were driven by a promise that a senior stakeholder had made and they were just wanting to deliver on it. I think there was a bit of ego involved there and saving face – and I get that. But the wider piece was the long-term reputational damage, the organisation just chucking something else over the fence – not understanding the needs of advisors. Which is something we heard more and more from the advisor network who were getting increasingly frustrated that the company were not helping them and didn't understand their business, which was incredibly scathing. It was a really important piece of work that really wasn't done well by pushing it through. Hannah

End-user engagement is lacking

I was called in because I was told that there was a morale problem in the IT project team. And after a morning of talking to them I said, 'No you don't have a morale problem: you have a failed project'. I worked with them for a year to 18 months. The project leader was one of these very clever, exceptional women and she got it in the first hour. Her eyes lit up and she said,

'I get it. We *haven't had the leadership required and the end-user involvement in designing this system.'*

So, the technical solution is problematic. Because the leadership team hasn't released the right person into the technical side and they then appointed a change manager, who set up a change agent network, and they redesigned the solution and launched again to great success. Erin

Key messages

- Not consulting sufficiently with end users.
- Choosing an inappropriate technical solution.

- Sponsors abandoning the project at the implementation stage.
- Measuring the success of the project too narrowly, i.e. on time, on budget, probity, but missing business fit and business risks.

11

ENSURING COMPLIANCE WITH NEW REGULATIONS

M any companies must change the way they work because new legislation requires it. In Australia, a Royal Commission into the banking and financial services industry made recommendations across governance, reporting processes and compensation systems. Change management objectives resulting from these recommendations have implications for organisational culture, skills development, leadership behaviours as well as organisational processes. The next change story concerns the introduction of a new code of conduct in banking.

Launching banking code of conduct

The launch of a new code of conduct at a bank impacted 75,000 employees around the world. This was by far the biggest change and communication project that I'd undertaken.

The launch of the code of conduct was successful. It

was sponsored by the CEO and had a deadline. It wasn't hard. It was a new code, a new policy – upping the importance of principles into a new code of conduct. However, sign-offs were complex for the company due to its size. That meant developing a contingency plan and stakeholder engagement.

It wasn't just the code of conduct. It had e-learning and needed to include the mandatory compliance module.

I wrote a book and I prepared a paper that was presented to the mandatory learning forum. I had worked with these people before, even though I'd only been at the bank for a short time.

Key for success was building those relationships quickly and establishing that you've got gravitas, i.e. that you know what you're talking about. It's fine if you are a bit junior and have a basic understanding, but the more experienced stakeholders are wanting someone who understands the business. Being in such a high-profile program makes the job easier because people understand its importance.

You've got all these stakeholders who are intrinsically linked but they are not employees.

You have to bring them all on the journey.

The Code of Conduct was more than a document. We needed to get people living and breathing the intent. We worked closely with the HR team, corporate comms, the CEO's office, learning and development and with the newly established cultural team, around culture and transformation.

It was led by a senior person within the compliance team. It was good having someone within the business driving it. He was driving through all the sign-offs for the code itself. He and I would work closely together. If I had a challenge with any messages then I would feed that back into the corporate comms team, and then they would feed that through the CEO.

Following up line managers to ensure people were doing the training

[Tell me about the consequences management framework]

If you mandate something and there are no consequences, people aren't necessarily going to do it. We had to work closely with the business owners, by having tricky conversations – they don't want to have these conversations. I would say, 'I can see that 70% of your employees haven't done their training. You have to get on to that', when they'd rather be talking about business development with their team. If you make it part of their KPIs then that's obviously helpful as well. It requires a lot of senior management buy-in to be successful. Hannah

Key messages

- Importance of project communicated by the CEO with a clear deadline for completion.
- Ensuring a senior line manager from a business line leads the project.
- Having a confirmed process for getting messages approved.

12

DRIVING CULTURAL CHANGE

Cultural change is perhaps the most complex type of change program as it involves changes to people's attitudes and behaviours. It can also take time. Culture is a big and complex concept and covers habits, behaviours, processes, attitudes, artefacts and is often described 'as the way that things are done around here'. Organisational culture can manifest itself in a variety of ways, including leadership and employee behaviours, communication styles, decision-making processes and office layout. While it can be hard to describe, culture is something you can feel after a short time within a new environment.

Change management objectives for cultural behaviour projects typically include steps to embed core values which manifest themselves in behaviours. Processes are sometimes created to support the behaviour change. Two stories that follow include one to embed a stronger safety culture and the other to support greater diversity in a male-dominated workplace.

Embedding a safety-first culture

Probably the first change program I was involved in was in the heavy resources sector. As a consultant, an engagement might be for a minimum of five years because they had a genuine commitment to driving a safety culture focused on building leadership capability, but equally around team performance and individual mindsets. This involved helping people to reframe how they viewed safety and why they would choose to stay safe.

There was a lot of focus on interpersonal skills and equally on understanding how the brain works, how we make decisions, and how we can make errors in judgment, how we can have very reactive conversations that go pear shaped, and how this impacts (from a safety perspective) when you're working underground. We coached leaders to help them to work with their teams, so they could adopt a different way of operating.

I delivered workshops that took people on a journey, but equally provided coaching, and psychometric assessments around their personal attitudes as they relate to safety, and then debriefing and helping them understand what to do with that information. From a culture change embedding perspective, leaders were coached to start every meeting to talk about safety by making it a conscious priority, even if the discussion wasn't safety related. This being a simple and powerful example of the values and commitment made to building a safety culture. Metrics are also key in culture change.

Organisations need clear and objective measures such as lost time injuries. Fiona

Achieving greater diversity in a male-dominated organisation

Many organisations recognise the value of building a diverse workforce because people from diverse backgrounds bring enhanced perspectives, stimulate creativity and enable better matching of customer demographics. Many organisations are also driven to achieve greater diversity in their workforce because they have values around inclusion of all. Diversity can be hard to achieve when employees are used to a certain profile of person in a role, such as a male engineer. Change management objectives for diversity projects typically cover recruitment, selection and development activities. Here's a story with diversity objectives.

I worked in a large, male-dominated engineering government organisation. The driver for a workforce with diversity was community pressure and a CEO who valued diversity. In achieving this goal, we faced resistance from a strong allied group of people who did not want this to happen and who were potentially protected by legislation. However, we were able to negotiate around this. There were concerns around us taking their jobs away. We shifted the conversation to

'Would you want your wife, daughter, your mum or your sister to be denied an opportunity? You know, your approach in resisting this initiative is alienating 50% of the workforce and indeed 50% of the population. Do you want them not to have this opportunity?'

Once the women had started in the workplace and

weren't given any special privileges, I think that's what made the change successful. Irene

Fostering a culture of innovation

Many organisations have recognised the need to encourage innovation as a way of ensuring their survival and success. While they can introduce systems and programs, building an underlying culture that supports innovation is much harder.

A few innovation-related stories were shared with me. These included start-ups dealing with early stage ideas.

Providing information and using the right language when explaining change impact

It wasn't until I started working with start-up companies and commercialising new technologies and things like that, that I could see a lot of similarities. For example, with start-ups and tech you're dealing with early-stage ideas. When we talk about change, we're talking about *user adoption* and understanding how people adapt to change: we always need to consider that.

[What information do they need in order to adopt something new?]

It could be either introducing a new technology or changing the way that a government agency operates, or the industry operates. There are a lot of similarities. Neil

Neil summarises the fundamentals in changing culture in government agencies.

> When we're doing capacity-building work within government agencies, you need to be able to explain the value of change, to allow people to assess whether the change is worth the pain and suffering. Whether that's changing processes, adopting new technologies, developing new products and services, whatever. Is it valuable enough to warrant the cost?

Key messages

- Long-term investments in awareness raising and training are required to drive change around safety.
- Build small conversations around the desired change into everyday work meetings.
- Have conversations that connect to the employees' own circumstances and interests as a driver for change.

13

BUILDING BETTER TEAMS AND LEADERS

The importance of effective leadership and dynamic teams has long been recognised as critical for success in any organisation. Indeed, the impact of poor leadership and dysfunctional teams has been widely reported by academics and consultants. Changing the behaviour of an individual or group can be hard. As a result, while change managers may design a broad organisational change program, they also need to engage in many one-on-one conversations. Many change managers come from a psychological or coaching background where these skills are frequently used.

In this chapter, the change stories cover use of feedback tools to build self-awareness, and understanding status and identity when teams merge.

Increasing self-awareness through use of a 360-degree feedback tool

There was this case of a huge gap between how the leader thought they were doing and how the team thought the leader was doing. His own boss and the leadership had nearly given up on him being somebody they could work with. So we used a 360 emotional intelligence assessment tool to raise awareness of how others perceived him.

[How does the emotional intelligence tool work?]

It's a self-assessment tool based on elements of emotional intelligence, so things like interpersonal skills, flexibility and stress management. You rate yourself and then you have other people rate you. The interesting thing is that you get a wealth of data that opens the door to a conversation. It's especially valuable for very irrational managers. The report shows the gaps between the person's perception and those around them and complements information collected from interviews.

On receiving the information in this case, the manager had two choices. He could say, 'Look, I can't take this', 'I'm not there' or 'I don't believe it and I reject it'. Or the manager could choose to recognise that how he dealt with this feedback was going to shape his future as a leader. He accepted the latter situation and with the support of a coach, the situation was turned around over several months. It took time as the manager needed support not to slip back to old behaviours. Kyle

A different story about change involves the merging of two teams in a council.

Building one team from two

I was engaged by a large department in local government to provide change management recommendations to support the successful merger of two very different business areas. Both business areas performed complementary work, and the business reasons were sound.

There was however a lot of history between the two, as this is not the first time this arrangement had been undertaken, and they very much considered themselves separate entities. Over the years they had been one division, then split, then brought together, then split. So there was a lot of history to work through in terms of the impacted teams being responsive to change, given their past experiences and perceptions.

While the work they performed was complementary, their backgrounds and skills were very different. In my experience, what is important here is to, firstly, understand the objectives and outcomes the senior leadership team are looking for, work with them to agree what success looks like, then through consultation, understand people's sentiment towards the change, and input for supporting the successful merger. This was facilitated through one-to-one conversations and group facilitation.

It's also important to acknowledge history and gain insights on what worked well and not so well previously, and use these insights to inform your change recommendations. It's much more about culture and ways of working than structure and process. Understanding culture and organisational behaviour is an important skill for change managers.

What I found out was at the heart of every change, people want to know:

- What I need to do.
- Am I going to be able to do it?
- What does this mean for me?

As a change manager, you are working with the leaders to be able to support people through the uncertainty and be able to talk about that future state in terms of why are we doing this. And the big thing we try and drive through the senior leaders is ownership and accountability for change in the business. We can only be as successful as the business taking accountability for their outcomes. You know, it wasn't a big transformation or anything like that, but it still had a cultural impact that needed consideration and planning to ensure the two areas transitioned effectively to achieve the desired business outcomes. Leanne

Key messages

- Provide support so people don't slip back to old behaviours.
- Build leadership confidence.
- When merging teams, understand the

background of those impacted and the
organisational history.

- Recognise that during change people want to
  know what this means for them.

14

WE'RE MOVING

Organisations can make physical changes to their workplace, or move their workplace altogether. While this change could bring improvements, it can also bring changes which are not welcomed by staff, such as a move to a hot-desking setup or an open-plan office. If the office is moved some distance and staff are required to travel further, this could have implications for staff motivation and retention. Other moves, such as the relocation of a hospital, can have a deep emotional impact given the history and staff connection to the old building.

Activities for this type of change are often focused around communication and engagement with impacted people, in addition to the extensive logistical aspects of the move. Impacted people include employees, customers and their families.

. . .

I want to share two snippets from change managers who worked on relocation projects before I look a little more deeply at the change implications of moving a hospital.

When three sites merge into one larger site

Different sites came together into this one super hub for this relocation project. Employees had a myriad of question regarding business operations and their personal impact such as:

'How do you pick up materials and drive your truck out?'

'What's the best place to park?'

'You mean I have to walk 500 metres now to get to the office?'

We provided an opportunity for everybody to have their say and explain that things are changing and the reasons why, based on facts. As an example, for safety reasons all non-work vehicles must park off site. We involved key people in the 'day in the life of a site' where they could understand what was changing and provide immediate feedback during the activity. Therese

Changed workspaces around the world to achieve cost savings

A global company employing 30,000 changed all their workspaces. It was not only a change to physical work space but a new way of working in an open-plan office. They had a very hierarchical business, a very status-driven business where having an office was incredibly important to managers.

The project was driven by cost saving. A massive transformation program across facilities' management as they renegotiated all contracts across the globe. The scope of the project including generating costs saving from everything from cleaning the toilets, to turning the lights on and cost millions of dollars. Ingrid

I heard several stories of office relocations involving a move to an open-space environment sometimes with hot-desking arrangements. A story at a hospital had this component along with many other changes. A brief description of the move along with learning is provided below.

Moving a hospital from one campus to another

We were not only changing locations but also the way the hospital operated. It was to be a completely new way of operating where a lot of people no longer had offices as we moved into open-plan arrangements.

The planning, communication and collaboration for the transition was done well.

We had mock trials of the move, with scenarios involving all stakeholders. Scenarios such as technology failures, patient incidents in transit, and physical issues were practised with external stakeholders such as the police and executive staff.

We employed people on the project with similar experiences for this type of move and had a project team office set up between the two sites.

There was a lot of attention and communication

placed on how awesome the new campus was going to be. However, what was overlooked until the end was that people had to say goodbye to a hospital site that they had grown up in. We had hundreds of people sharing memories of events via a massive LCD screen running 24/7, to acknowledge these memories and to allow them to say goodbye.

Keys to success on this project included

- Daily stand-ups. Regular working group meetings across all the clinical specialties.
- Lots of face-to-face communication. One of my colleagues set up a biweekly change chat, which was basically a meeting with coffee.
- Fantastic public relations team, who let the community know about the hospital closures and patients being moved.
- A patient-centric view and making sure that the impact to patients and their families was minimised and the quality of care wasn't compromised.
- Implemented a multi-dimensional communication plan.
- Used technology for community actions. The IT guys set up an application to bring together all information flow and logistics so that we could track staff having ID cards and making sure they had access to the right customers; making sure all new phone numbers had been correctly allocated; ensuring staff knew where their muster points were on day one.
- Sophisticated reporting enabled us to work with

the various business owners, reporting on what
had been done and what still needed to be done.

- Understanding the rhythm of the business and
  adjusting the change and communication plan
  accordingly.
- Communication from trusted sources. Recognise
  that people don't want to hear from project teams
  and the change manager. They want to hear from
  their managers, supervisors and people that are
  in the trenches with them. The most powerful
  thing that we can do in change management is
  identify those influencers and support them.
  Helen

Key messages

- Don't underestimate the loss of status and
  identity when moving to an open-plan
  arrangement.
- Listen and respond to staff concerns through the
  most credible channels, and create effective
  planning and reporting processes.
- The hospital relocation highlighted the impact of
  the move on the local community and the
  importance of communication. A few people
  shared stories about when this important
  community consultation was lacking. Insights
  from projects needing better community
  consultation in the next chapter.

15

WHEN COMMUNITY CONSULTATION IS LACKING

C hange programs can impact staff, customers and other external stakeholders. External stakeholders are not always easy to identify and their reaction to the changes could negate the intended benefits of the initiative. This is particularly relevant for government. Two examples in this chapter include construction of a new tunnel that the local community did not want, and the unknowing removal of trees planted as a memorial to soldiers killed in the war.

Cross City Tunnel in Sydney

This project connected the east and west sides of Sydney, delivered through a public–private partnership with the objective of taking traffic off the surface roads to reduce congestion.

The technical side of the project was ambitious and involved connecting with three other tunnels, through sandstone, and figuring out entries and exits. It was successful, being delivered before time and on budget. On the people side, the tunnel generated massive resistance to change with people blockading the streets. People who had used particular roads would no longer be able to use them – and they were angry.

The project went bankrupt within 18 months. It was sold and went bankrupt again. Sydneysiders never accepted the change. Today people will still drive 5 kilometres out of their way not to use the tunnel. Erin

Accidental removal of sacred trees

I was working on a street renewal project in a regional town for a council, which involved removing a few old trees and replacing them with a new planting.

I hadn't been involved in the early days of planning and it didn't occur to me to ask,

'Where did the trees come from?'

It turned out that they had been planted by members of the community in the forties to respect those involved in the war. There was nothing on the trees identifying this.

By the time the local community raised concerns, the trees were gone and they'd been mulched. There was going to be a boycott of all the shops in the main street. This is a small regional town, so it was very traumatic for anybody not to go down the main street. And they we're going to go to town council meetings and let everybody know how uncaring council was.

Nobody at council knew who had planted the trees and assumed council had done it. If we had known earlier and engaged these people, they still would have been unhappy but we obviously would have had a better outcome such as transplanting the trees or installing a plaque.

There was a public apology in the local paper but it was really awful for a long while.

I learnt that you need to sit back, identify your stakeholders and survey everything before you start planning anything major. Irene

Key messages

- Community consultation is paramount for public change projects.
- While you can achieve technical and project management goals, you can fail to achieve user acceptance.
- You may have important and unidentified stakeholders for your project: make sure you take the time to identify and consult with them.

16

CRISIS-DRIVEN CHANGE

C hange programs can be broadly classified into two types: evolutionary or revolutionary. Evolutionary programs are introduced, as the name suggests, over time while a revolutionary change program is often crisis driven, with the very life of the organisation at risk. As I noted in the introduction to THE JOURNEY, revolutionary change is often driven by a challenge to an organisation's survivability. This creates a great impetus for change. In his book *Leading Change*, John Kotter talked about the 'burning platform' which gives the change project a greater sense of urgency.

Change management objectives for these urgent projects typically include keeping the organisation financially viable or getting a start-up successfully launched. Here are a few quite different stories touching on start-up failures, a need for fast decision-making, and when there's a history of things being managed badly.

Trying to get lift off with a start-up

I was involved in a pretty spectacular start-up failure. Mainly because the senior managers were very focused on what they wanted to achieve rather than what the technology could do. So personal influence started to impact and stop things from happening. They decided that they needed to have the right image and focused more on what their salaries were going to be rather than on what validation was required from the customer. Thinking too big, trying to change too quickly. They were always after the really big customers – the big projects. They had this view that doing the small stuff was a waste of time.

I see a lot of challenges within corporates because managers are used to making decisions with a 90–95% confidence level. Any decision that a manager is making is based on a fair few facts. Then you get a new bit of tech and there's a fair few assumptions around it and it can be hard for managers as they don't have the facts they're used to having to make decisions.

From an innovation perspective, you need to understand what business-as-usual means. You have an idea for a new product or service that is to become part of the whole product or service offering. What information is required to make that occur?

Most corporate innovation systems aren't geared around that. They are geared around finding and assessing ideas and seeing if the tech works, rather than focussing on information that marketing or production needs. What information do they need to say, 'Yes, this is our next product and this is how it's going to be rolled out'? When you start focussing on what information you need, then you design a different proof of concept process. It's no longer around collecting data for tech, it's collecting data for the decision making purposes – to convert that idea into the next generation product or service. It's a different way of looking at change management. That's why I see the link with commercialisation, innovation and change management. Neil

It goes without saying that crisis-driven change is driven by a desire to avoid failure. Insights on political and decision-making challenges you face during this period are revealed in the this next snippet.

Business is in financial trouble

If you're battling politics or too heavy a level of bureaucracy, you will not win. Because it will be too slow and you will always be deferring to someone else. You can't move. When you can't move quickly or decisively enough or you're seen as being really slow in solving problems, that will impact on the confidence of people in the organisation. You need to be clear that we have a beacon where we are heading and we are going to get it done. Nigel

When a business fails, redundancies typically follow. Managing this process well can be difficult. I heard horror stories of people being communicated with via text or suddenly discovering that their access to the office has been denied. But I also heard positive stories as you'll see in Zadie's snippet below.

Laying people off

> I've seen organisations who've had to lay off people. They do it so well because they've been really transparent and explained why they need to take some action. And people accept that things can't stay the same. Maybe they resign themselves to the change, but they won't actively resist it if they are given the context.

A good example of explaining the context, and for treating people with dignity and support during a layoff came from AIRBNB while I was writing this book. (You can read about their messages and process at www.news.airbnb.com.)

Sometimes organisations have a history of managing people badly during difficult times. Our next story highlights the implications of previous programs that were managed badly.

When the previous change program was badly managed

> Because people go through moments, they vent. People just want to vent. I find more and more that for change that has been done badly, at some of my workshops, they end up being counselling sessions for the first 30 minutes

to an hour, as they talk about the organisational memory of previous poorly done change.

And they just need to tell you, and there's no getting past it. If I focus on the positive future, you get stuck. I'm like, you can't get to the positive future because they're so frustrated, angry, upset by the last change, and we need to let them talk and vent. And then there comes a point, where you use your judgement or intuition and say,

'I think we've reached a limit now – we're not hearing anything new in the venting. Now, it's time to say "Line in the sand. Let's go forth"'.

It's an acknowledgment of emotions, and from here we can move on with what we want them to do. Ingrid

Key messages

- Recognise that we have more assumptions than facts when introducing new products or services.
- There's a need for fast decision-making processes in a crisis.
- Change managed badly in the past can be a barrier to future changes.

So, we've reached the end of the JOURNEY stories. We're now all going to sit around a metaphorical campfire and reflect on what we've learnt and think about what happens when we leave.

PART III

AT END OF JOURNEY

17

WHEN I LEAVE

I left the organisation and later ran into the consultant who was supporting us in delivering this work, which was going to touch thousands of people and there were already other departments signing up, and he said to me, 'Oh, ever since you left everything fell flat'. (Fiona)

A change manager's involvement in any project will be time limited. They could leave before a new system goes live, or the new way of working is embedded so that there is a return to the previous way of working. Or all the right behaviours are adopted but there is a turnover of staff who are not given the briefing or education that had been provided to those they replaced.

A few reflections and stories follow, highlighting what sometimes happens when the change manager leaves.

When the project ends and the change managers go away and we try to measure to see if we are sort of getting close.

And at some point, we arrive and then the people that were supposedly changed are all relieved and immediately revert back to what they were doing before. Ken

Staff turnover impacted on new processes

One of my interviewees told the story of setting up a safe environment for play at a child care centre and how a lot of the process changes reverted back after she left.

> I was asked to set up the kids' club at a new hotel in Indonesia. I did things like advise on the fencing around the fish pond and asked for the removal of a slide into the pool as it would be too hot for children during the day. I also wrote an operational manual, describing safe processes, and designed and ran a training program for staff.
>
> A year after the hotel opened, I was invited back. I could see that the 'nuts and bolts' of what I'd put in place were still there but because of changes in staff, the recommended processes weren't being followed. Western customers at the hotel don't want their kids watching TV all day. They want them engaged in learning and doing activities. And when they are doing an activity, you can't do it for the child, no matter how imperfect it looks, you have to let the child do it for themselves. And getting those messages across wasn't easy. And when I went back a year later, there were still some of the same behaviours. Elaine

The toll of digital transformation on staff

One interviewee reflected on the impact of change programs on those driving it as well as staff.

I was just speaking at an event with our staff and a question was asked referring to the 'digital cliff' that would occur at the end of the transformation program. For three years we have been delivering solutions for the business, but there was a concern that it was all going to fall over when the contractors walk out the door. How would they continue to evolve these minimum viable products that had been delivered? How would they be supported? I said no, no, no. Firstly these products that have been delivered – MVP or not – can stand on their own. They're a bike. They've got wheels. If you want to put streamers on the bike add big mirrors, we can still continue to do that, but we will do that over time, through both our "as a service" contract arrangements and our internal staff who have also been along this change journey and have learnt the necessary skills along the way.

Our program has been like climbing Mt Everest with nine people dying in May 1996 - with metaphorically the same challenges - it's about agility, mindset, planning and being prepared to change when circumstances change. But that takes a lot out of you and a lot out of key people, so building and maintaining resilience is also an important. Oscar

Building capability in the change champion network left behind

Our viewpoint is that we leave behind capability. We're equipping people. Even on the really big changes, we should be able to pull back – and staff there pick up that this is the new way of working. We run Change Management 101 course covering how to be a change leader, those types of things. We obviously set up our little change champion work groups where it makes sense and give them different techniques, that type of thing. Samantha

Key messages

- There is a risk of reversion in behaviours when the project ends and a new *business as usual rhythm* is in place.
- Consideration needs to be given to the things that will support the new way of working once the change managers leave.
- Going through a major transformation program takes a lot out of people.

18

MEASURING EFFECTIVENESS OF CHANGE

When the project is completed, it's important to review the measures identified at the beginning of the project to see if they have been met. There's always learning to capture from both the successful and less successful initiatives. I asked all interviewees how they measure the effectiveness of their change programs.

Measuring changes to safety culture

As a leading consultancy in safety culture, we adopted a few different measures. One was conducting a safety culture assessment, prior to actually commencing the engagement and then again at the end. We assessed individuals' attitudes to safety, and looked equally at anecdotal feedback that came from leaders around what they could see changing within the organisation.

There were lots of good news stories where people mentioned somebody who had been quite resistant, and all of a sudden, there was this, almost like a switch had gone off and they had completely shifted and started to become more engaged in becoming more of an advocate, in terms of working safely.

We undertook regular surveys and had a high completion rate – which is also a sign that the project is going well. We combined surveys with face-to-face consultation. Fiona

No negative pushback in the media and talent retained

We delivered it within the timeframe that needed to be delivered. Funding was secured. We demonstrated that the changes were in place. We retained the talent that we had identified as needing to be retained and we didn't get any negative pushback in the media. We were able to sit at the executive table with the sponsors who said, 'You guys equip us'. They said yes when we needed to send out a letter with their signature. Samantha

Measuring standard metrics rather than change metrics

As a project manager, I don't really measure change management as such, but I measure key metrics on the project – you know – time, costs, quality – you know – standard things. And I think I'd be making the assumption that all the project activities, including the change management, they're judged against how well we're going against those measures. I know the change managers do have their own measures and some of those will involve things like user surveys that at points in time check in with the people, and see what the position is at one point, and then check again to see if things have improved and you're getting the outcomes you want. Lionel

Reporting on change readiness and change challenges

It's important to establish change metrics early. These need to be relevant to the outcomes you want to drive, and should be around adoption and the employee experience, i.e. how ready people are for change, and how supported they feel. These metrics are very different than the usual project metrics of on-time or on-budget delivery. It's about ensuring the right metrics are in place to measure that people are adopting new ways of working, embracing new technology and effectively performing as a result of the change, and ultimately the organisation is realising the benefits and outcomes they set out to achieve.

We work with the business to establish and track these metrics through reporting to the senior leadership team. As a change manager, how you influence in that space is important. Otherwise, how do they define the success of a project? Is it about delivering on time or is it about people using new technologies or adopting change and not reverting back to old ways of working? It's that benefits realisation piece. Some questions that you can explore with the appropriate leaders and stakeholders include:

- What's the impact of this change?
- Does it impact the whole organisation, or does it hit across a small part of the organisation?
- How many people? The entire organisation, a few divisions, or one team?

- What are the change risks associated with it?
- What is the change leadership capability of the people leading it?
- How will we know we are successful? What will people be doing differently? Leanne

Business measures and relationships

The HR team were looking at best fit, productivity and stakeholder and media issues.

They collected a lot of data that showed the cost to serve. From a business perspective, the first thing they looked at was business results. So, from a quarter-by-quarter perspective, how is the revenue impacted or not impacted by the integration process?

So that's probably the first thing everyone looks at, and the results are actually very good. The company grew through change integration, which is very rare. Wayne

Key messages

- A range of business, project and behavioural measures can be identified and tracked to enable the impact and effectiveness of a change initiative to be demonstrated.
- These stakeholder measures could include qualitative information such as anecdotal feedback, and quantitative data such as user adoption, while business measures could relate to revenue or business growth.

19

CHARACTERISTICS OF THE BEST CHANGE MANAGERS

In Australia, demand for change management has outstripped supply. It's probably the same in project management. It's a big challenge to recruit and develop capable change managers. And I guess that will always be the case. As we get more mature and as the profession grows, we need people who are capable and experienced and who can work across different organisations.
(Erin)

It's not about being the sage on the stage; instead, it's about being the guide on the side. (Therese)

People come to the change management profession and learn their craft by many different paths. They could come from project management, organisational development, training or communications roles, to name a few of many paths. As I was curious to learn what distinguishes the good from the great change managers, I asked all interviewees, **'What are the characteristics of the best change agents?'**

I've summarised their responses into three categories: Attitudes/Behaviours (Table 1), Knowledge (Table 2) and Skills (Table 3). Explanatory comments by the interviewees follow the tables.

Table 1: Attitudes and behaviours of the best change managers

Relationship	Gravitas	Perspective and insights	Attitudes
Empathy. Calming influence. Empowers others Good at relationship building (Quickly) Compassionate and open minded Resilient and can foster resilience in others Team player	Credible with senior managers Builds good relationships at all levels in organisation Creates trust Professional. Has credibility and gravitas Possesses charisma. Has presence Possesses confidence to negotiate solutions	Can see the big picture Admits mistakes Curious – insatiable thirst for knowledge Flexible and adaptive Brave and courageous. Not afraid to try Comfortable with uncertainty and ambiguity Knows when to leave the client alone	Invests in lifelong learning and knowing themself Inclination to innovation and agile Possesses a learning mindset. Curious Like a professor. Is humble

Table 2: Knowledge of the best change managers

Methodology	Project management	Understand data	Business related experience
Doesn't use a standard approach Knowledge of tools and methods Recognises that change management is different in every organisation Understands different frameworks such as Prosci or Kotter Able to design a bespoke approach Possesses toolkit of useful things like stakeholder maps Understands culture Understands stakeholders	Ensuring resourcing for the project and risks around the changes are understood Understands the difference between a risk and issue Good time management Comfortable with measurement	Understands requirements, data testing and traceability Understands conversion rates and sentiment analysis Has experience with systems rollouts	Has broad experience and knowledge across companies Understand other disciplines Governance practise

Table 3: Skills of the best change managers

Communication	Skills development	Politically aware
Communication planning	Identifies training needs	Politically astute
Is articulate. A storyteller	Understands how training and knowledge acquisition works. How you acquire knowledge and apply it?	Can build political support and identify saboteurs
Able to explain the value of change		Resilient
Asks the right questions. Good listener	Good workshop facilitator	
Able to have difficult discussions	Good one-on-one coach	
Being proactive and responsive		
Emotional Intelligence uses appropriate language		

Resilient. Flexible. Adaptable.

Things change. Scopes change. Patience is needed. The reason why I say patience is that for some organisations, their maturity of change is very low. And we have practitioners with a high level of change maturity who get frustrated going into an organisation with a low level of maturity. I remember one practitioner saying 'That it is all well and good when you talk about best practice and high performing teams, but in my organisation, they don't even know how to communicate, before we even think about change management'. So my response was, 'Why don't you start there? Change isn't about your experience. It's about where they are, at their maturity level. Sometimes you need to drop your expectations because all you want to do is to get them to go one level up'. Carrie

Credible with senior managers. Establishes rapport. Knows how knowledge is acquired.

They've got to be able to talk to leaders at very senior levels. Identify who those people are. They can't just rely on, 'The PM will tell you who to talk to'. They have to be able to identify key areas and key problems. They have to engage with that person, to develop a rapport. So when they tell me about the impact assessment, I want them to tell me that out of this analysis should come clarity on what we need to communicate with people. I ask,

- What strategies did you put in place?
- How did you actually do that?

Then I might slip into how they put communications together. And then I want to know how they've identified training needs. Do they understand how training works, how knowledge works? I believe that training is a great background for all change managers. You need to understand how you acquire knowledge and what you do with it. Lyn

Planning. Resourcing. Risk management.

What good change managers do well includes communication planning, working closely with the project manager to ensure that the risks around the changes are discussed and understood. Ensuring that the resourcing for the project management activities – in terms of not just the people but also the budget – all that is in place and we have what they need to implement the change plans. It's very much operating as a project manager might operate, but there's other elements to a skillset as well. I'm thinking in particular about things like empathy and understanding, which are critical for change managers. These are often the skills or characteristics that project managers don't necessarily have, or don't have enough time to apply. Lionel

Professional. Able to read people. Calming influence.

Wrapped up in one word, professionalism. They know their craft and the processes they need to follow. Good at capturing information. Stakeholder maps drive the contents of a change management plan. It's quite technical, understanding what needs to go in there. And then the softer skills around the empathy and understanding, the ability to, I guess, read people and just to understand where they're coming from and then translate that into a plan for managing their concerns. That's a really good soft skill. Not everybody's got that. A lot of project managers don't have it either.

Having a calming influence as well when there's a lot of change happening is important. It doesn't have to be chaos.

I see change management as a risk management activity. And I talked about those discussions that you might need to have with senior stakeholders to tell them. Oftentimes they have difficult discussions and you have to get messages understood to get support. Framing it in the context of risk as a project manager is usually pretty effective. Lionel

Understands business needs. Good facilitator. Emotionally intelligent.

People who are respected for their expertise and can understand the language and needs of the business from the business leader's perspective, and can influence those leaders with what they are trying to implement. Goes beyond having expertise. If you can't influence, it won't work.

Being an engaging workshop facilitator. Not just sending out information, but getting people to practise whatever the thing is they need to do.

Possessing a toolkit of useful things. Practical things, like stakeholder maps.

Helping people feel empowered with the process of change.

Having a degree of Emotional Intelligence or EQ and using appropriate language. Here's an example of someone with poor EQ using language that would frighten people.

During a radical restructure that was going to result in some people not having a job, a new person in charge of this area came to two different teams on different days and opened the conversation saying, 'If you all died, if you blew up in a plane crash, and I was reading your obituary what would it say?' Elaine

Project management. Pitching. Perspective.

Other things are around project management. Knowing what are the benefits we're after.

What are we going to do to achieve them? Making sure people know where we are on the journey. All the basic project management skills. Communication skills. Having fun. To be able to laugh even if it's a high-pressure project. Being able to make the case for change. Elaine

Explains value of change. Collaborative design. Understands root problems.

When we are doing capacity-building work within government agencies, you need to be able to explain the value of change, to allow people to assess whether the change is worth the pain and suffering. Whether that's changing processes, adopting new technologies, developing new products and services.

- Is it valuable enough to warrant the cost?
- What's your understanding of the high-level problem and the root problem?

You can have interventions that target high level problems that will generally work for a little while but they will eventually fail because the underlying problem is not understood.

Things that worked well with this project included:

- Good design
- Good understanding of what the problems were
- A solution developed in conjunction with stakeholders.

They were taken along on the journey and it was explained to stakeholders how they would feel through the process. Letting them know that there would be periods when they would feel completely out of control – and that these were normal feelings. So when you explain the change process and the feelings behind that, when stakeholders and participants feel that, they know that it's normal. If people don't know this, they react. And the easiest way to respond is to go back to the way they were doing things before. Neil

Politically aware. Good listener. Comfortable with ambiguity.

Being politically aware in overseas jurisdictions: the consultants had to be without prejudice. Make sure they are there for the right reasons – so screening was really important.

Good listener. Respectful. Understanding the benefit of having different people's ideas.

Able to deal with uncertainty and ambiguity. Possessing confidence to negotiate solutions in areas of uncertainty. It's very rare to come up with something black and white. They need to be comfortable with ambiguity as there is always grey.

Possess and foster resilience in others. Understanding people's reactions and how they deal with change. Are resilient and can foster resilience in others. Resilience comes from being comfortable enough with change. Neil

Open minded. Creative problem-solver. Understands other disciplines.

Are compassionate and open minded. Having practitioners that have multi-disciplinary backgrounds because they are experienced at solving problems in more creative ways.

Practitioners need to understand the difference between a risk and an issue and the difference between a bug and an enhancement. I think if you're working in technology, you genuinely need to understand the data testing process as well, because having an understanding around requirements, traceability and having a business analyst [BA] to support you and to translate a lot of that. I think if you're not comfortable, then you need to be reaching out and working more closely with your BAs, but to understand what's in the requirements, and when you're going into testing and people going, 'It doesn't work'. It's like, is it that it doesn't work here, – that it was built correctly in the first place, documented and it was built for what was documented – but that was foundationally wrong?

I think having a high-level understanding of what goes on in other disciplines helps us to think differently, and allows us to be the effective advocates for end users. Helen

Curious. Insatiable thirst for knowledge. Not afraid to try.

Having that natural curiosity to look for different ways to facilitate and engage is important. If I think about some of the best change managers I know, they have an insatiable thirst for knowledge and just finding new ways to break through with stakeholders. Interestingly enough, a lot of them have gone into positive psychology and neuroscience. They are not afraid to try.

I also think there's a difference between an intermediate practitioner and a master. The master is prepared to make mistakes and learn from things that haven't worked rather than being paralysed with a decision. Helen

Able to empower others. Has a flexible mind and is a good communicator. Is not afraid. Lina

Doesn't use a standard approach.

The thing that bugs me is we're starting to develop this really almost a manic approach to methodology that doesn't accommodate for organisational culture and maturity. Change management is not a *paint by numbers* approach to doing things. Helen

I am firmly of the belief that there is process – but every project and program is different. Don't have a cookie cutter approach. Hannah

I've seen change managers come in with copy book stuff, theoretical stuff. It doesn't fit with our particular stage in the program, or division or issue. They need to be respected by the business people. Oscar

Understands business. Proactive in looking for opportunities. Credible.

They are very good at understanding our business and culture deeply. They are continuously looking for opportunities. Oscar

Has fluency in different core business functions. Edouard

Really key is establishing gravitas, and early on. Because stakeholder engagement and leadership alignment can make or break a project. You need the trust of these people under an incredibly aggressive timeframe. It's not calling in favours but people are going to be much more willing to provide feedback quickly, if you can explain it in the right way. Not only do you need to understand the end-to-end business itself but what's important for each part. What's going to help them? They understand the pressures that they are facing. What's keeping them up at night and how can you help them? How is the project going to make their lives easier? Hannah

Leadership. Builds trust. Politically astute.

The best leaders build trust. They are empathetic: listening, reporting back and relationship building. There are times when they need to be very directive, saying, 'This is the way we are going'. A bit of selling, a bit of telling and a bit of coaching. And it's working out where people are on that change journey. Leaders set out the vision, 'The Why'. People need to understand why things are happening. In large organisations there are political considerations. You need to be politically astute. There are often more enemies within than outside the organisation. People can white ant you. You need to have people watching your back. Nigel

Sometimes it's hard to identify the active saboteurs because they're often not in meetings. So you've got to spend time triangulating those meetings. Zadie

Strategic. Practical. Knows when to change approach.

Having a clear strategy and program underneath the strategy to roll out. Being prepared as we run agile, to change as new things emerge.

You can read a book about change, you can theorise about it, but what's the greatest for me is being able to apply that in a practical context. Those three or four things all come together. Being able to listen and understand the business. Being prepared to be agile in change – and having that strategy and program clear. Oscar

Communication channels, coaching capability and calling it out.

Use multiple channels for communication and many times. Similar or same message because not everyone gets it the first time. You need to communicate with the right people at the right time and don't raise unnecessary expectations. There will be people in the organisation who want to know everything about everything – and we say no, you only need to know this information at this time to do your role. This allows us to ensure the message is clear and they understand what we are asking of them or their 'job to be done'. Oscar

I rely on my coaching capability: to frame the straight talking with empathy. Being able to talk through things and pull people up as well, because sometimes they've never been pulled up. I question, 'Why do you keep saying that about yourself? And why do you keep saying that about the other person there?' And it's they're like 'What do you mean?' Therese

Understands complexity. Is eclectic. Has a diverse toolkit.

Because change management is complex, it looks different in every organisation, because of what you're trying to change in the strategy, objectives and culture and leadership style in that organisation. What makes a great change manager is to be quite eclectic in their approach. You obviously have different tools and methodologies and I don't actually align with any in particular.

You'll have those who go out and do all the Prosci stuff or now we're applying Kotter's methodology, whatever that might be. And yes, you can go through the motions and tick stuff off. But I don't think that's what achieves successful change results. And I think in fact, that is one of the things that leads to change efforts failing. It's when you just have this one tool, this one change methodology. It's a proven methodology: there's a ton of research and every other organisation and change managers using it. So you use it. I think having a breadth of experience in different organisations, using a variety of tools and investing in your own professional and personal development is critical. Fiona

Scans external environment. Voracious learner. Empathetic.

I've personally always been very, very conscious of understanding what are the changes that are happening in the world and in different industries. I've done lots of things and invested in executive development programs, in coaching, in culture change and in design thinking. I just think you can't stop. And what happens is you try and test things, and then you have your own natural style and know what works for you.

And I think empathy is the other piece that's critical, that emotional intelligence, because you're constantly dealing with people, and it can be emotionally draining. At the end of a week, you can feel super tired and not know why. 'Cause you've just sat through a series of meetings. Empathy is necessary because if you're not able to demonstrate to people that you understand them, there's no way in hell that they're going to come into the conversation authentically and engage. Fiona

Broad range of experience. Invests in their development.

Great change managers have a broad range of experience working within different organisations and industries, and across many different types of change. They learn from their experiences, are curious, and continue to invest in their own professional development through on-the-job learning, peer-to-peer networking and keeping informed on best practice insights through their research and other development activities. They have a large change toolkit and know which ones to use when. Change management is never a 'one size fits all'. They also understand other relevant and complementary methodologies and how you can align them with change management, including organisational development, leadership development, agile ways of working, innovation and design thinking. Digital transformations are also a space that benefits from experience working in this context, so staying abreast of trends and best practice is recommended. Leanne

Works well with people across disciplines. Designs bespoke approaches.

I think they need to be able to operate and engage with a broad range of people. I've been in organisations where you're working with tradies and engineers, right through to very technical and non-technical people. You need to be able to build relationships with people from a base grade right up to senior leadership. It's important to be a people person. You need to be very strategic, especially when you work in the transformation space. You also need to be agile and design fit-for-purpose change management interventions, because you can't just come in and think that what worked at another organisation is going to work in the next. Leanne

Assertive. Able to manage difficult conversations.

Change managers bring unique skills and experiences to an organisation. It's important to be confident in your own ability and the value you bring to the table. It may also mean being assertive and comfortable in having difficult conversations. Leanne

Like a professor. Is humble. Talks about their own mistakes.

And I sometimes see change managers and they're more like professors. And it's nice. It's nice to be a professor because it's such a different power dynamic. The really good ones I also see are very humble. They easily talk about their own mistakes and their own journeys. And that brings you down to a level with customers where you're not this guru, but you're one of them. And that meant that sometimes it's difficult for people, because in your mind, you submit your status and your expertise. Kyle

Understands governance. Knowledge of data testing. Ability to interpret data.

We need to understand the difference between program and project governance. We need to understand the environments in which we operate and the general cadence of a project governance cycle.

If you're working in technology, you need to understand data testing and interpretation.

We've got good assessment and analysis tools at our disposal to capture and review behavioural insights. Conversion rates and the sentiment analysis allow us to refine what we do and identify *unspoken truths*. Some people seem to be so focused on open rates and click through rates and they look at what's apparent rather than what's not there. And if you're sitting there understanding what it is you're trying to measure and looking at who is engaging is great, but it's understanding who's not engaging and unpacking why. Helen

Confident. Curious. Establishes relationships quickly. Project management background.

As I said before, empathy. They need to be confident. In case we get push back from people.

People who have come from a project background, so they've worked in a project as opposed to operational environment. They are often a bit more attuned as to how to deliver. Because change is a series of deliverables as opposed to operations.

People who have a generally curious mindset can deal with change. They are quite flexible in their mindset and the way they like to work. They need to be brave and courageous.

If people are only going to go in for a short period of time, then they really need to be able to establish relationships quickly.

For me the best change managers are certainly not those who are saying I have to go to my next job at five days a week. This is what it needs to look like and this is where I need to be. I'm looking for change managers who are looking for jobs for 18 months to two years. You need to be able to stand back. If you're in there for too long you lose that. Samantha

Articulate and able to write coherently. Outgoing personality.

Definitely having people who are quite articulate is important.

You need to write a fair bit, so you need to be able to express yourself in a way that doesn't lose people through use of jargon. Communication is the art of being able to get your message across to a diverse audience – in a way that doesn't incite fear but creates curiosity and still delivers. It's a bit of an art. Samantha

I've always thought that the school teachers make great OCMs because they've got that brilliant dose of empathy and energy and interest in educating someone, and taking them on a journey: building an understanding of what the end state looks like. Damien

Intuition mixed with experience. Sees the big picture and the detail. Outcome focussed.

People will make a decision about you in 30 seconds. So you have to be able to have people to hang in there long enough to listen to what you've got to say. I would say the ability to scan the environment and know when something is off. And whether it's something you need to do something about or something you can let go and wait and see.

I would probably call that intuition, mixed with experience. And I would think that that same intuition and experience is what then makes you say, 'This client, I need to use these tools for this process'.

An example of that would be we all do engagement, it

could be workshops, that maybe with this particular client in their culture with how they like to do things, we should be using more design thinking. I should be doing codesign, you know, as against a more traditional workshop, because it's collaborative. But I think you've just really got to pick your tools to your client.

I would say that you need to be a good communicator and time manager. I hear a lot of complaints about change managers who don't deliver what they say we're gonna do. There are a lot of people who just have nice conversations. This is not enough. You've got to deliver outcomes.

I think you have to have an ability to see the big picture and also drill down into the detail.

And this is my very personal opinion. I think that different change manages are good at different parts of the change management process. I'm very much an upfront person. I like doing the change strategy, understanding your organisation, getting the sponsorship model in place, getting people ready. And then I've worked with other people who are the implementors. I'm just in awe of them. But they had never written a change strategy in their life, and have no interest in writing one. They want to be handed the plan. Ingrid

Team Player. Able to analyse and synthesise qualitative data. Understands culture.

Need to be a team player. Is happy to analyse, synthesise, and create some kind of theming or plan out of the data. We get a lot of qualitative data in our jobs so you need to be able to come up with observations or anecdotes that gives the client confidence in what we've done.

A good change manager knows when the project is going off the rails. You get this sense. Your intuition tells you that this is not going to end well. Your clients could be concerned about what stakeholders are doing. And you're watching them, and you're like, 'You know what? No, just let's just leave them be for a minute, I think it's gonna come good'. And it does. It's that kind of thing. You got to also know when to leave them alone.

I think understanding culture. If you can't understand the culture then I can't see how you can be successful. Ingrid

Can 'read' stakeholders.

It was such a political environment that it was critical for change practitioners to be tenacious about reading stakeholders so they can work with them in a way that gets results. It's not always easy because there's a lot of people that say one thing and do something completely opposite. And you don't have a lot of time to build the rapport or address behavioural issues. So you have to stroke a lot of egos. And I think without that ability to really read those senior stakeholders, it would probably have been a disaster. And some of those things I'm referring to are things like backstabbing and bad mouthing and not committing to what they agreed on, and actually creating another coalition to go against the committee. Wayne

Structured and results oriented. Balances the hard versus soft part of change

Having a structured discipline is critical. A lot of change managers are very good at talking to people and managing stakeholders but don't have a structure for driving things to achieve results. At the end of day, we're working on projects or initiatives, and there is a beginning and an end. We need to be able to demonstrate and talk through a set of approaches and activities that go from A to B. And it's quite common for us to have change managers who lack that. They usually just took you through, well, we're going to start with a change plan, change assessment, all these activities, but that doesn't actually describe the approach.

And the second thing I would say, is a balance between the hard and the soft parts of change. I can't tell you how many change managers I've met who've told me that they're only in change management because they like to work with people. And they don't want to spend time doing measurements, you know, the quantitative aspects of change.

And for me that's quite a challenge when you're not able to talk to change results with your key stakeholders. I mean, having said that, yes, you need the soft skills around having to read audiences, how to work with teams and all of those skill sets, but the hard skills around measurement, tracking, business results, and structure and frameworks are just as critical as well. We need to demonstrate results from every part of the change.

And I've been in companies where they've said, 'We

don't have much budget, we're going to get the BA [Business Analyst] to do the change work instead'. Because it's really tough to see the value, but then if you're coming to the table by demonstrating that this is what we did, here are the business results, then you're really actually demonstrating the value of change management.

The other thing is, I think a great change practitioner needs to have that clarity and cut-through to say, 'Okay, this is the situation, these are the topics that we need to be doing, and this is how we're going to do it', versus just listing a series of activities that just become business as usual. It's all about how we get from A to B without losing focus.

Being able to work through the lens of what the business is going through rather than having a myopic focus on one project because in the business world, that's just one of many projects. Wayne

Has presence. Experience counts. Tells it like it is.

What I mean by *presence* is that if there's a crowded room, somebody walks in and whether they have an aura – invisible or real, whatever it is, I don't know – but people will look at this individual or people. You need it, because you're dealing with the full spectrum of people from the board of directors and steering group down to operational people. So, you need to be recognisable.

The other thing from a more tangible perspective is about people getting certified or not. I have to say this because I've been around a long time and I think experience counts. What makes you a change manager is that you been at the coalface. I personally can't see somebody who has little or no knowledge of change before they go on one of these change management programs is going into managing a fairly large change project. Broad understanding of all the different models that are out there is valuable. You need to understand Prosci and you need to understand Kotter etc. And you need to be able to use that information to build what I call a bespoke approach. Gaining the trust of the people that you are representing.

Don't be shy to tell the powers-that-be, such as the steering committee, in simple straight language but with evidence. Some people are reticent to state their true opinion. They always try to skirt around some of the issues and paste over the cracks. Don't make it nice, because if you don't tell it the way it is, you know, you're doing a disservice to yourself. Neville

Good at building relationships at senior levels. Designing interventions. Storyteller.

These people are very good at building these really good relationships with people high in the organisation avoiding HR and corporate purchasing and all of these people who put up barriers. They are also extremely good at delivery and truly gifted when it comes to building interventions and coaching. Kyle

I think a change manager is like a conductor of the orchestra. It's you bringing so many different parts together. And getting them all together in the right place. Being able to build that vision for people. Being maybe a bit of a storyteller and having that vision to help people see the picture.

They've gotta be a people person. They've gotta be prepared to put their hand up and say, 'So I mucked that one up', taking accountability and responsibility for what's going on.

Talk to people acknowledge their concerns, but not give in to them. Sometimes you've just got to fight the good fight. And that doesn't mean you invalidate their concerns. You can acknowledge them and recognise them.

You also need a bit of a thick skin at times, and believing in what you're doing. Irene

Being clear about your role. Valuing everyone's time.

In my very early days, the senior executive wanted the change manager to be there for everything and I thought, 'Do I need to be at everything?' Part of my role is to facilitate and to drive an outcome, so planning is important for every interaction to ensure the purpose is clear.

I look around the room and place a dollar figure on everybody sitting in that room because that's the value of having all those people together for whatever that purpose is. I ask myself, 'Are we ensuring people's time is wisely invested in this meeting?'

It's necessary to use your coaching skills to gather leader views and knowledge where complex changes cross multiple divisions and teams. It's getting the data in such a way, to position it and say this should be both the plan that we could present moving forward and be able to change as well. I used to work with a PM who said, 'You just deal with the fluffy stuff'. And I said, 'This fluffy stuff is hard work and I'm putting together a plan based on all these bits of information, to support people who don't ultimately understand what the change is, leaders who can't articulate it, perceptions of gains and losses and I'm trying to piece that all together,

'Right. I'll give you fluffy stuff.' Therese

Closing remarks

I know this has been a longish chapter. There are so many competencies required of a successful change agent and I loved the rationale provided by the interviewees. I can see that many skills and attributes mirror those required in any leadership role, such as seeing the big picture, understanding how organisations work and having good communication and relationship-building skills. There's also a string of personal attributes that are critical such a self-knowledge, willingness to admit mistakes, and gravitas with senior managers as well as front-line staff. For large scale change projects multiple practitioners are often required. Let's briefly look at the characteristics of great change teams.

20

CREATING GREAT CHANGE TEAMS

Depending on the project, you may be in a change team with project managers, technical and functional specialists, business analysts, communications professionals, trainers and change roles that are similar roles to yours. You could be working directly for the organisation as an employee or undertaking a time-limited project as an external consultant. Your team members could be located physically near you or in another country. You could also have created a coalition of support roles such as change champions who aren't technically in your team, but are a critical part of your network.

For large change projects, practitioners often work in teams. I was interested to learn more about the best change teams. In this chapter I share observations covering how teams are constructed, the physical location and organisational position of the change team, and how to build and sustain team members.

Construction of teams

[Can you tell me a little bit about the team? Who else were you working with on this one-year project?]

We didn't have any consultants, it was a small team, with myself and a few US colleagues from corporate development. Together we came up with a structure of what we wanted for this integration team and created a working group and the project teams by region.

And then we used that structure to execute the overall project. There were probably about ten or eleven senior stakeholders at the regional level, with all functions represented.

It was really great and I think that in project situations, a lot comes down to how people work together within the project team and it's often overlooked. I think that's a core role of change practitioners who have a natural skill set in terms of relationships, people and behaviours, and of ensuring good team dynamics within the project team. Wayne

When there's a small change team

I think most of the change teams I've worked on have been extremely lean for the size of the organisation and change that needs to be done. And by working through those key stakeholders in the change network, you're able to expand your reach, focus on the coaching and the support. Helen

Physical location of change manager

A couple of practitioners mentioned the importance of the physical location of the change manager in terms of influence.

If I see a change manager or transition manager that sits like in an office, like in a head office and is never outside, I'm pretty confident that that person is not going to be having impact. Kyle

We find internal talent as soon as possible within the organisation who we partner with. We absolutely have a viewpoint of leading from behind and making sure we find people who can join us. It also influences where we sit. There might be a project team off to the side in the freezing cold under the air-conditioning space. We ask, 'Can we sit with you guys?' Samantha

Importance of alignment and consistency of approach

As change managers, we all come with different experiences, approaches, ways of working and preferences for the type of change work we enjoy. Understanding this from the outset and agreeing as a team how you will work together and how you will deliver change management services to your business stakeholders to ensure they experience a consistent service is important. This also supports the organisation building their own change management capability through this shared experience. Leanne

Regular communication

I cannot overemphasise how important it is to regularly
communicate and reflect on experiences as individuals
and also as a team. The most effective teams share, learn
and grow together. Leanne

Build and sustain a trusted network

I think you need to have your trusted network. I'm lucky
enough to have great colleagues. Even though we're quite
different in the way we approach things, we ultimately
share the same goals in supporting the business and
leading change. I'm the lead here, but absolutely respect
the experience of my two colleagues. Leanne

A great change management consulting practice is one
which does what we preach. I had the opportunity to join
such a consultancy when it was still relatively small,
consisting of around 20 people. This company lived and
breathed their culture and has since grown to 150 people.
Very much about doing, no matter what; whatever we
preach, we do it ourselves. So we'd literally shut down
business for two days every two months, with no client
meetings, phone calls, client interactions or emails. These
days would include one day dedicated to professional
development and the other to fun. And that fun was
surfing, wine tasting, cooking classes and breezy lunches,
whatever. It varied. And doing that was recognising that
you need to have a very strong and collaborative team to
be successful.

So, we lived and breathed the culture. And I still remember the values around professionalism and integrity – and I cannot tell you the values of any other organisation I've come into contact with. That's how powerful it was. And the values drove the decisions that we made.

Values not only influence decision making, they drive behaviours and change managers' behaviours will be closely observed. Fiona

This point was reinforced by Helen.

We will be modelling the behaviour. We will model the behaviour of the change we want to see.

Ask smart questions when recruiting

I was talking to the lead today, and she is about to go out and recruit some change managers. I asked her if she knew what question I asked that immediately tells me if the interviewee understands the change process. I eliminate 80% of people with this one question.

'Tell me how you did the impact assessment in this project? What was the process you used?' Lyn.

Key messages

- Change practitioners should ensure that there is a great dynamic within the change team itself. As a result, the team should spend time together on professional development and team cohesion activities.

- The physical location of the change manager or team inside the client organisation will impact on their visibility and influence.
- We've reached the end of the journey. It's now time for reflection, to look at the learning and pull a few final reflections together.

21

PULLING THE LEARNING TOGETHER

*Those that have experienced the big projects that have gone off
the rails, know about the value of having focus on the people side
of things. And they are so dubious at the beginning. Or so cynical.
They say, 'Oh you're doing the easy stuff?' So I laugh and reply,
'Don't you mean the hard stuff?'* (Ingrid)

We started this journey by considering what change management is. Many definitions talk in terms of travelling from point A to point B or transitioning from a current to new way of working. We talked about the process for getting people comfortable with uncertainty and building their capability to be ready for the change.

Change projects could be driven by organisational mergers or restructuring, new technology, new legislative requirements, cost-saving initiatives or a desire to change the culture of the organisation. Each type of change will require an approach suitable for the culture and legislative environment within which the organisation operates.

If you're embarking on a difficult project it's important to consider the organisational environment and the likely challenges you'll face. These challenges could be from anticipated or unanticipated stakeholders, or from the normal political machinations inside the organisation. Make sure you build your alliances throughout the organisation and come packed with both resources and skills, thinking about the journey from both a people and a systems perspective. There are many resources to choose from: the best change managers know which approach and tools to recommend, based on the culture of the organisation and the scale of change required.

A change manager could come from backgrounds including organisational development, project management, business analysis, systems implementation, communications or training to name a few. Keys to success however are not so much the background but the understanding of how organisations work, a capacity to build relationships and to get things done inside a project management structure. They'll possess outstanding communication and coaching skills and have the confidence and gravitas to lead difficult conversations, as Therese highlighted.

Here's a great opportunity while all these changes are happening. You can step up into leading this change and show people what you are capable of. A part of that is that change brings opportunity. How do we have that conversation when people hear that things are changing?

The best change manager has an *always learning* mentality and will build reflection and knowledge capture into their everyday processes. This was evident in comments such as this one from Lionel.

With hindsight, I would spend more time with the senior management than I would with the people impacted by the change, to be honest, to get them more directly involved.

As Ingrid has highlighted at the top of this chapter, it's a tough gig being a change manager. Research and stories told in this book show the many ways that a major change program can go astray. However, there is much to learn from the stories shared within these covers: I hope that you've picked up ideas on actions you can take to increase the likelihood of success.

22
_____

THANKING CHANGE STORIES
CONTRIBUTORS

I n writing this book I was motivated to learn more
from the experience of others. *Change Stories* is a
collection of their stories. Without them, this anecdotal, story-rich book would not have been possible. My
acknowledgement and thanks go to them for their insights.

> *Alan Sparks*
> *Anne Crowley*
> *Brian Ruddle*
> *Catherine Smithson*
> *David Christmas*
> *Eleni Jurkschat*
> *Euan Wu*
> *Huibert Evekink*
> *Jacqueline Davila*
> *Joanne Rinaldi*
> *Joanna Wyganowska*
> *Kellie Dyer*
> *Kerryn Fewster*
> *Lesleigh Ross*

Liz Henderson
Liz Short
Michael Morahan
Michelle Ross
Nick Emery
Ron Leeman
Ruth Hine
Simon McKee
Stephane Malhomme
Susannah Graham

PART IV

RESOURCES PACKED

I n this final part I provide a dictionary of terms often used when you work in change management and a brief description of the tools and methodologies mentioned by the interviewees.

FAVOURITE TOOLS, TEMPLATES AND PROCESSES

I t was *not* my intention in writing this book to discuss the myriad of processes, tools and templates that a change manager carries in their metaphorical tool kit. I told all my interviewers that I only wanted to hear their stories. Well, as things go, tools, templates and processes were frequently mentioned in our interviews so I decided to include a section here mentioning the ones I was told about.

Some of the favourite resources are described next.

Causal Effect Modelling are mathematical models representing relationships within an individual system or population which facilitate inferences about causal relationships.

> When I was running design teams, I would have technical people with me, that were jumping to the solution very quickly. Part of my job was to stop that and to say that we are not yet at the point. We need to keep analysing the problems. Because when you keep analysing problems

more deeply, you see what you thought was the problem may not have been the problem. Neil

Competing Values Framework, developed by Robert Quinn and Kim Cameron, provides a classification of four corporate cultures, giving insight into how a company operates, how employees collaborate and what the corporate values are.

Design Thinking/Human Centred Design has a deep focus on understanding the people, (or users) for whom the products or services are being designed. It uses an iterative process to understand users, challenge assumptions and redefine problems, and is most useful for tackling ill-defined problems. It has five phases: Empathise, Define, Ideate, Prototype and Test.

> Helps you to focus on employee experience. Takes you through the phases including developing personas of different employee groups, mapping the moments that matter and then developing a prototype. Elaine

Excel is a spreadsheet developed by Microsoft, typically used to organise data and perform financial analysis.

Impact Analysis

The key thing is that any tools that I use, such as impact assessments, I do this in collaboration with the business. I facilitate the questions. They give me the answers. I consolidate the impacts, then I put together the graph, or the proposal or the recommendation based on their results.

They tell me what the current state looks like and I interpret it. Because if I do this by myself with a template on a computer, then I have to justify the results. If it comes from them, all I am doing is interpreting.

I have an 80/20 rule. 80% of the time I am working with the business, collaborating and engaging, and 20% is representing the plans and strategies based on that collaboration and output.

Whereas if I spent 80% of my time doing my own assessment, then I have to justify how I got the numbers and everything else. And it defeats the purpose. Carrie

McKinsey's Seven S Model is a tool that analyses an organisation by looking at seven key internal elements: strategy, structure, systems, shared values, style, staff, and skills.

Microsoft Teams allows team conversations, files, meeting creation, and apps to be together in a single shared workspace, and you can take it with you on your favourite mobile device.

Net Promotor Score is a tool that measures customer experience.

Get all data and then calculate the NPS [Net Promotor Score]. Publish it to everyone. Here's what we think about ourselves. It's a very important indicator. Nigel

Obeya is a lean concept that focuses on setting up a physical space where you strategize and plan your projects. Obeya helps you to generate ideas, collaborate with management and stakeholders, and gain a full overview of the projects and any problems that need to be resolved.

Obeya means big room in Japanese. The idea is to bring people involved with all parts of a production process into one place so that they meet face to face to improve communication and prevent compartmentalising or phasing work to homogeneous departments. Lyn

OCI is an Organisational Culture Inventory that shows how employees interact with each other, what they have in common, and what is expected of them in terms of behaviour. Behavioural standards influence productivity and effectiveness in the long term, as well as the engagement of each employee individually.

OCAI (Organisational Cultural Assessment Inventory) is a cultural assessment tool based on the Competing Values Framework and is a quick culture tool where you distribute 100 points between four *Competing Values*.

Is a good tool for cultural analysis. Lina

Prosci is a change management methodology developed by the consulting firm of the same name. Prosci's model of individual change is called the Prosci ADKAR Model, an acronym for awareness, desire, knowledge, ability, and reinforcement.

Pulse check is a short, quick survey that is sent out to employees on a regular basis. It is essentially a check-in, providing a *pulse check* on topics such as communication or employee satisfaction. Usually its limited number of questions makes it quick and easy to complete the survey. It can be a key measure of employee attitudes during change programs.

> We used pulse checks. Their managers were constantly communicating the changes to them, to get them on board, what it means for employees to do what they do throughout the change. What I mean by that is, that it's not just to communicate with them, but to engage with them. Ingrid

Questions to ask during assessment

What causes that? This is a simple cause and effect thing. It is simple, but it is starting to unpack what people mean by things. We spent a lot of time trying to understand terminology.

Which processes do we follow? For a number of clients, we would find that they don't follow the stated process. They may follow another process to that which is written. You need to get to the nuts and bolts. And I often use this process when I'm working with start-ups.

I say, 'I've got this piece of paper. Walk me through this paper. Show me how this works. **Who signs here? What happens there?**' What people say they do what they do and what the problem is, often isn't the case. And they're not lying. They just don't think that this little thing over here makes the difference. Neil

RACI Chart is a matrix of all the activities or decision-making authorities undertaken in an organisation set against all the people or roles. At each intersection of activity and role it's possible to assign somebody responsible, accountable, consulted or informed for that activity or decision.

SCARF Model involves five domains of human social experience – status, certainty, autonomy, relatedness and fairness – and how these affect (for better or worse) human interactions.

Scenarios. If you talk about a likely or possible scenario, you are talking about the way in which a situation may develop. You can then think through how you might respond.

I was really strong on trying to find people that could deliver quality, and we used scenarios that were revealed through role plays. They'd never done this before to my knowledge. Ingrid

Stakeholders and Decision Making. A stakeholder is a person or group who is affected, either negatively or positively by successful project completion.

> I'll send that out to make sure the key stakeholders are across it, I'll meet with them if I need to talk it out, looking at some of the board minutes which make it look like it was a really short discussion. Here was the issue. Here was the decision. The paperwork behind it is where the detail is. Most people don't want to read the details. But the project registered decisions within an Excel-based tool. It doesn't matter what the tool is. We have a registered system and we record the key decisions and then we've got documentary evidence with the detail around what the issue was, what the options were, what the decision was. Lionel

Steering committee is the most senior decision-making body on a project.

There was a steering committee, with representatives from the different areas and we had regular sessions with project updates for about nine months. Neville

.   .   .

Survey Monkey is an online survey tool that enables the creation and management of professional online surveys.

Systems Thinking is a holistic and analytical approach to organisational analysis that focuses on the way that a system's parts interrelate.

> One thing that we haven't talked about is systems thinking. You are actually dealing with systems in most places and there is a need to understand the components of those systems. This links back to your previous question about who is involved. I've seen 'blocking' happen in the weirdest areas. Say you're getting near the end of validating a new product or service in a large corporate and there is a decision to engage the marketing division.
>
> They have their KPIs that have nothing to do with this new tech and they'll block it. It's one of those things, but if you understood that they were part of the system, and the development process took into account that they were an integral part, then you would have been engaging with them earlier, and finding out that that was going to occur. So we put in place processes to deal with these types of things. Neil

LANGUAGE OF CHANGE. ACRONYMS. ABBREVIATIONS. GLOSSARY OF TERMS

My partner doesn't work in change management or indeed in the corporate world. And I love it because I say things sometimes, and he goes, 'I'm sorry. I don't understand what you're talking about.'
(Ingrid)

Here's a little dictionary for Ingrid's husband and anyone else who wants to understand the change management lingo.

360 or 180 degrees tools – multi-rater feedback tools through which feedback about behaviour can be sought from an employee's subordinates, colleagues, and supervisor(s), as well as from self-evaluation. The data is analysed and presented in a report given back to the individual.

Agile – an iterative approach to project management and software development

. . .

BAs – Business Analysts

BAU – Business as Usual. Sometimes written as BaU

CRO – Chief Risk Officer

Bleeding Edge – used with reference to new technology that is at the forefront in its field

Digital Transformation – the integration of digital technology into all areas of a business

DMAIC methodology – Six Sigma approach. Design, Measure, Analyse, Improve, Control

Due Diligence – a comprehensive appraisal of a business undertaken by a prospective buyer

EPO – Enterprise Portfolio Office, an organisation-wide approach to project management

EQ – Emotional Quotient; also referred to as emotional intelligence

. . .

Enterprise PMO (EPMO) – a centralised business function which operates at a strategic level with the enterprise executives and provides enterprise-wide support on governance, project portfolio management best practices, mentoring, tools and standardised processes

HR – Human Resources

Innovation – bringing a new idea into existence, e.g. a new product, service or process

IT – Information Technology

Kotter Change Model – an eight-step framework for driving change

M&A – Mergers and Acquisitions

MNC – Multi National Company

MVP – Minimum Viable Product. (Also, MVS for Minimum Viable Service)

NPS – Net Promotor Score is a customer loyalty metric

·   ·   ·

OCM – Organisational Change Management is a framework for managing the effect of new business processes, changes in organisational structure or cultural changes within an enterprise. It focuses on the people side of change management. The term is often used interchangeably with change management. OCM practitioners, as opposed to a project-specific change manager, work on organisation-wide change projects.

OD – Organisational Development, a speciality area within human resource management considering change from a people and organisational perspective.

Operating Model – determines how the business delivers value using people, process and technology. It is a way of mapping (or representing) how an organisation interacts with its customers or beneficiaries. It is often represented as an abstract image with boxes and arrows and can appear in strategy documents.

Project Management – the practice of leading the work of a team to achieve goals and meet success criteria at a specified time.

RACI Chart – a matrix of all the activities or decision-making authorities undertaken in an organisation set against all the people or roles (See 'Favourite tools, templates and processes' for more information.)

· · ·

Prince2 – a process-based method for project management.

PMO – Project Management Office

Resistance – in a change management context, relates to individuals and managers pushing back against the changes being proposed or implemented.

SERCO – Service Corporations, operate public and private transport and traffic control, aviation, military weapons, detention centres, prisons and schools on behalf of their customers.

Shared service model – where services are pooled in one part of an organisation and shared with other parts of the organisation. The funding for the unit is shared and the unit becomes an internal service provider. Change managers are sometimes located in a shared services pool as opposed to being allocated to one part of an organisation.

Sponsor – the person or group who owns the project.

Sustainability – the ability of an organisation to continue its mission or program far into the future.

· · ·

Transition – Change involves moving from a current to a future state with the transition referring to the messy middle part where people are having multiple reactions to the change. Transition is often used in the context of people's reaction and reorientation to the change. A transition management plan is a component of a change management plan.

Walking the Talk – behaving in a way consistent with the values you espouse.

Waterfall projects – where requirements for the software/system are clearly defined at the beginning of the project, unlike agile projects where project scope evolves iteratively in response to feedback.

REFERENCES AND FURTHER READING

I n case you want to know more.

Anderson, D. & Anderson, L. A. (2010). Beyond change management: How to achieve breakthrough results through conscious change leadership (Vol. 36). John Wiley & Sons.

Kotter, J. P. (2012). Leading change. Harvard Business Press.

Machiavelli, N. (1961). The Prince (1532), trans. Angelo M. Codevilla (New Haven and London: Yale University Press, 1997), 65.

. . .

Ross, L. (2020). Change management: The Essentials: The modern playbook for new and experienced practitioners. Lena Ross

Turner D. & Crawford M (1998). Change Power: Capabilities that drive corporate renewal. Business and Professional Publishing. Warriewood. NSW.

Web Site references

How long can your company survive?
http://www.ft.lk/columns/How-long-can-your-company-survive/4-653904

The Hard Side of Change Management
https://hbr.org/2005/10/the-hard-side-of-change-management

OECD and Governance
http://www.oecd.org/corporate/principles-corporate-governance/

ASX Corporate Governance Council
https://www.asx.com.au/regulation/corporate-governance-council.htm

. . .

Change Management governance by Linda Ackerman Anderson

https://blog.beingfirst.com/creating-effective-change-governance-for-your-change-initiative-whos-in-charge-of-what

Changes in Technology

https://www.cio.com/article/3404876/what-does-digital-transformation-really-mean.html

Meaning of building capability

https://www.brandlearning.com/views-ideas/latest-views-ideas/learning/is-capability-building-a-fancy-name-for-training-and-if-not-what-does-it-mean/

AIRBNB messages

https://news.airbnb.com/a-message-from-co-founder-and-ceo-brian-chesky/

ABOUT DR TRACY STANLEY

I started my career in global companies including Xerox and British Airways and later joined Amadeus. I was fascinated by how changes were made across the business in multiple countries and cultures.

I spent five years as a change manager on a global customer relationship management deployment project, five years leading organisational development projects, four years in knowledge management, and two years as an individual transition coach.

When I came home to Australia after many years abroad, I was surprised by the proliferation of short-term change management vacancies, often asking for skills in digital transformation. I wanted to know more. This is what prompted me to write this book of change stories.

. . .

My previous books include:

Engagement Whisperer: A quieter and more collaborative approach to inspiring your team team

Creativity Cycling: Help your team solve complex problems with creative tools, co-written with creativity expert, Barbara Wilson

Always keen to learn, I've acquired a few qualifications including a Master of Business (Research), MBA and a PhD. My doctoral research considered how work environments impact on creative behaviours and employee engagement.

Apart from writing books, I blog. You can read my musings on life in organisations at http://tjstanley.com/articles/

You can also find me on the following **social media channels.**

- Facebook
  https://www.facebook.com/Engagewhisperer/
- Twitter @tjstanley64
- LinkedIn https://www.linkedin.
  com/in/tracystanley1/
- Bookbub
  https://www.bookbub.com/authors/tracy-stanley

- Pinterest https://www.pinterest.
  com.au/tjstanley64/
- YouTube https://www.youtube.com/channel/
  UC98owLf5k5GWEjWGgus-7vQ
- Goodreads https://www.goodreads.com/author/
  show/18989774.Tracy_Stanley
- Instagram https://www.instagram.com/
  tjstanley64/?hl=en

I write a monthly newsletter about what I've been learning about organisational change, creativity, innovation and employee engagement. You can read them at the link below and sign up by popping your email in the box.

http://tjstanley.com/newsletters-learning-creativity/

If you have your own change stories to share, I'd love to hear from you. Email: tracy@tjstanley.com

And finally, if you've obtained insights from this book, I'd value a review. (They're like gold for writers!) You can send it to me directly at tracy@tjstanley.com, pop it on www.goodreads.com or wherever you purchased *Change Stories*.

Thanks for listening and all the best with your efforts to drive change in your organisation.

Tracy

ABOUT CREATIVITY CYCLING

I n a fast-changing world, new challenges frequently arise. Complex problems benefit from creative thinking revealing new perspectives and opportunities.

Creativity Cycling: **Help your team solve complex problems with creative tools** provides an overview of the conditions for creativity, both individual and team, and presents a tried and tested process for solving complex problems and envisioning the future.

It is written for leaders who want to enable their team to work creatively in responding to complex challenges.

Authors: Barbara Wilson and Tracy Stanley

. . .

To be innovative and competitive today brings demands on teams to adopt a continuous improvement culture. To nurture this requires rigorous methodologies of creativity, innovation to generate new solutions to problems whether it be for internal improvements or market-facing products.

Creativity Cycling is a handy, quick to consume reference bringing together a range of proven techniques and practices for teams to consider at different stages of ideation. This book provides a simple and well-structured introduction to the benefits of creativity and improving the working environment across your teams with some understanding of constraints to consider.

What others have said about *Creativity Cycling*.

As I run a lot of strategy workshops at different levels, I found this book valuable as it provides a range of low fidelity tried and testing methodologies to have at hand when you need to ideate or open up problems. I now have it quick at hand in the office for a handy go-to reference. Craig Strong, Global Speciality Practice Advisory Lead for EMEA

I was so impressed with this book by two well-respected practitioners and researchers. The layout and use of colour keep readers engaged and help leaders and facilitators to dip back in to find the activity that will work for their group. Theory and research are balanced by practical suggestions that encourage leaders to find new ways to encourage their teams. Free of jargon, business-

speak and academia-speak. Desolie Page, Owner of Perfect
Pages

ABOUT ENGAGEMENT WHISPERER

Many writers have highlighted the business value of deeply engaged teams. Indeed a great team is powerful, much more than the sum of its individual people. While many things influence engagement at work, and indeed there is complexity – it isn't rocket science.

Engagement Whisperer: **A quieter and more collaborative approach to inspiring your team** demystifies the science and describes a 'softly, softly' approach to lifting engagement in your team.

There is already so much noise in an organisation that a quieter approach might just be the right 'cup of tea' (or coffee).

.   .   .

Learning for managers is distilled in thirty delicious and easily digestible bites. It's designed as a dipper or a flipper. Simply, you can read a chapter or two at a time on the bus or while enjoying a cappuccino (my preferred option).

The book is targeted at managers in large organisations and draws heavily on PhD research into what's happening when people are highly engaged at work. The results are recommendations for manager's behaviours and team processes.

There's also a chapter discussing what it's like to live in a large organisation and how this influences your status and identity. The book is sprinkled heavily with the voices of employees.

The book will also be helpful for those with responsibility for organisational wide employee engagement initiatives. Perhaps you are in human resources or corporate communications. There is a chapter written with input from folk who have run these programs.

The book is a fun and enlightening investment of a manager's time. You will come away with ideas on things you can do to support your team members engagement at work.

What others have said about *Engagement Whisperer*

Really enjoyed the book. Loved the practicality and quiet ways of doing things. There are little tidbits of things we can all incorporate into our management styles that can have big payoffs. Its maximum bang for your buck too – more than value for money. Kym, Amazon Five-star review

This book does a fabulous job of educating about engagement in the workplace and how to help employees become more engaged. Dineace Minnick, Amazon Five-star review

Dr Stanley's book is a valuable resource for managers in large organisations as it reveals the characteristics that most engage people and provides practical advice on how we can create conditions to bring out the best in our employees. Dr Monique Beedles, Managing Director Teak Yew

Tracy cleverly brings together the dos and don'ts for creating engaging workplaces. A must for managers who want to get the best out of their teams and themselves! Huibert Evekink, CEO Futureteaming

This thoughtful and practical book dispels the myths that 'engagement' happens because of glitzy, once a year initiative. It's a relief for those who can't offer curated workplaces complete with ping pong tables, free lattes and bean bags adorning the ubiquitous 'chill-out zones' where the magic happens!

Tracy's work shows that real and sustained engagement comes from a more thoughtful and human centred place; a place where respect, trust, fairness and personal growth sit at the core. Engagement is now demystified and accessible to all. It should come with a product warning: putting these practices into action may put you under the spotlight. Expect to be asked for your recipe for team success or leave your peers secretly wondering if there is something in the water! Wendy Lundgaard, Principal Consultant/CEO of Win-Win Workplace Strategies

REFLECTIONS

I love a blank sheet of paper (or two). So I've provided a couple of pages here for you to jot down your notes with a few questions to prompt reflection.

What have I learnt about successful change programs?

What experience and skills do I need to acquire to become a more effective change agent?

What frameworks, tools and methodologies should I learn how to use?

Who should I talk to about their lessons learned to become a more effective change practitioner?

My next books to read include ...